MODERN
Handfasting

About the Author

Liz Williams is a science fiction and fantasy writer living in Glastonbury, England, where she is codirector of a witchcraft supply business. She has been published by Bantam Spectra, Tor Macmillan, and Night Shade Press, and she appears regularly in *Asimov's Science Fiction* and other magazines. She has a long-term involvement with the Milford SF Writers' Workshop and also teaches creative writing. Williams is a member of the Order of Bards, Ovates & Druids and has been working for many years within the British occult community, including organizing the annual Glastonbury Occult Conference.

a Complete
Guide *to*
the Magic *of*
Pagan Weddings

MODERN
Handfasting

LIZ WILLIAMS

Llewellyn Publications • Woodbury, Minnesota

FIRST EDITION
First Printing, 2021

Cover design by Kevin R. Brown
Cover and part page illustration by Dominick Finelle

Llewellyn Publications is a registered trademark of Llewellyn Worldwide Ltd.

Library of Congress Cataloging-in-Publication Data
Names: Williams, Liz, author.
Title: Modern handfasting : a complete guide to the magic of pagan weddings
  / Liz Williams.
Description: First edition. | Woodbury, MN : Llewellyn Worldwide, Ltd,
  2021. | Includes bibliographical references.
Identifiers: LCCN 2021027614 (print) | LCCN 2021027615 (ebook) | ISBN
  9780738766584 (paperback) | ISBN 9780738766829 (ebook)
Subjects: LCSH: Handfasting. | Marriage customs and rites. |
  Marriage—Religious aspects—Neopaganism.
Classification: LCC GT2690 .W55 2021 (print) | LCC GT2690 (ebook) | DDC
  392.5—dc23
LC record available at https://lccn.loc.gov/2021027614
LC ebook record available at https://lccn.loc.gov/2021027615

Llewellyn Publications
A Division of Llewellyn Worldwide Ltd.
2143 Wooddale Drive
Woodbury, MN 55125-2989
www.llewellyn.com

Printed in the United States of America

Other Books by Liz Williams

The Ghost Sister

Empire of Bones

The Poison Master

Nine Layers of Sky

Banner of Souls

Darkland

Bloodmind

Snake Agent

The Demon and the City

Precious Dragon

The Shadow Pavilion

Winterstrike

The Iron Khan

Worldsoul

Comet Weather

Blackthorn Winter

The Banquet of the Lords of Night

A Glass of Shadow

The Light Warden

Miracles of Our Own Making: A History of Paganism

The Witchcraft Shop Diaries (1 and 2)

Forthcoming Books by Liz Williams

Embertide

Salt on the Midnight Fire

Dedication

To Trevor Jones, my fellow celebrant and partner:
the only person I have ever handfasted, and the only person I ever want to handfast.

Thanks to everyone who has contributed their stories for this book and to all
the people who have trusted us to undertake their handfasting as celebrants.
It has been an honor and a pleasure.

Contents

Prologue

The hillside is sunlit, but there's a touch of rain on the wind, and the rowan berries are already a deep scarlet. The distant road is fringed with the spires of rosebay willowherb, the color of an emperor's cloak, and beyond, the blue Welsh hills vanish into a misty distance. The priestess glances up, a little anxiously. It's always an unpredictable country for outdoor rituals—but it would have been the same in the ancestors' days, over two thousand years ago, and we're not far from the ancient monuments of the Preseli hills, where some of the great stones of Stonehenge were mined. Far away, the sea is a silver line. The priest joins the priestess, asking, low-voiced, "Have we got everything?" She nods. Everything's ready. Ahead, through an arch of willow, she can see the stump of oak that, today, will serve as an altar.

The first guests are starting to straggle up the path. Some of them have nervous smiles: they're not all pagans. The bride's friends are a combination of Wiccans and Druids, but the groom's family don't really follow any religion, and they don't know what to expect. The groom has told his mates with a straight face that there might be a ritual sacrifice, and although they don't actually believe this, it's sufficiently far out of their comfort zone to make them a little bit twitchy (with some added hilarity, too). They're gathering on a Carmarthenshire hillside on a Saturday afternoon rather than being down at the pub for the rugby, but they're laughing and joking anyway. The bride's friends, who will be calling the quarters, are also coming up the path, wearing medieval dresses and garlands around their hair. They look lovely, and they've made a big effort, but they're not as nervous as the lads. They've all done this before, and they're looking forward to it.

"All right," says the priestess. "I need everyone in a big circle, around the altar. Yes, that's it. That's great—thank you." Meanwhile, the priest is ushering the bride and groom from the willow arch to the altar. On the opposite side of the field, facing east, lies a broomstick. The bride, in a billowing golden skirt and bodice that she has made herself, and the groom, in a pirate shirt and black jeans, smile at one another and at their friends.

The priestess crosses to the altar and raises a silver chalice to the sky. As if on cue, the sun sails out from behind a cloud. "Welcome to the ancient rite of handfasting, which we're conducting today for Rhiannon and David. We're going to tell you a little bit about what we're going to do here today, and then—we'll begin."

Introduction

In this book, we will be taking a look at the many aspects of handfasting—the custom of pagan marriage. Handfastings are a magical occasion, your special day in which you and your beloved set the seal on your love for one another in a ritual ceremony. We will look at the different facets of handfasting: its history through the ages in the British Isles and Ireland, and its evolution into the range of contemporary pagan ceremonies we know today. Handfastings now are celebrated across the world—you will find couples from Vancouver to Melbourne who have been handfasted. We will examine the legality of the ceremony in different regions and how you will be able to legally marry as well as be handfasted. In addition, we will look at the practical aspects of handfasting (how to find a celebrant and choose a venue, for instance) and, in the second half of the book, the ritual and magical elements in this kind of ceremony. You will learn how to make a handfasting cord, create your own incense, and write your vows. Handfastings are not necessarily a complicated ceremony to organize, but there are a number of things to think about. My aim in this book is to answer as many of your questions as possible, both pragmatic and magical, and, finally, to leave you with a sense of confidence that your big day will go as smoothly as possible.

I am a celebrant myself. Together with my partner, Trevor Jones, I have conducted over a hundred handfastings, as well as rituals like baby namings and funerals, over the last twenty years. We have spoken to many couples who choose to mark their commitment to one another in this fashion, and over the years, we have come across (and resolved!) many of the common problems that handfastings may present. I do not just draw upon our own experience and expertise, but on that of other celebrants. Our friends range from Wiccan elders to Church of England clergy and live in places as diverse as Orkney and the Netherlands. Some work as professional celebrants, while others have simply had a handfasting themselves. All of them have been generous with their time and knowledge, and you will find their words of advice throughout this book. Tips for the celebrant will be found at the end of relevant chapters.

Many people who seek out handfastings nowadays are not themselves pagan. As celebrants, my partner and I have handfasted many people of all religious backgrounds, although a large percentage of them are pagan (at least one of the couple follows a pagan path, for example). Increasingly, the ceremony is seen as a humanist variant, without the formal and perhaps rather stifling trappings of a traditional, conventional ceremony.

Where do we begin when it comes to handfasting? What's the history of this wedding ritual, familiar to modern pagans now for over half a century? Where and when did handfastings begin? And how do you go about organizing one?

In this book, I will try to answer all these questions and more. We'll be taking a look at the following:

- The history of handfasting
- How to find a celebrant
- How to organize your ceremony and advice for brides and grooms
- Will you need a handfasting planner or wedding organizer?
- Advice for celebrants
- Taking part and advice for guests
- Where and when
- The magic of handfasting
- Making your own ritual tools
- The handfasting ritual
- Honoring the gods

- Writing your vows
- Troubleshooting

And we'll be including personal experiences from celebrants and hand-fasting couples, too.

I use the terms *brides* and *grooms* throughout this book, but I need to stress that this applies not only to heterosexual couples, but to any couple who wants to become handfasted. I have officiated at many same-sex handfastings in addition to ceremonies in which one or both participants are transgender and/or nonbinary. It is really up to individual couples whether they want to use the terms *bride* and *groom*, and if not, that's fine. Raven Kaldera and Tannin Schwartzstein's book *Inviting Hera's Blessing: Handfasting and Wedding Rituals* includes a ritual, the rite of Aphrodite-Urania, specifically for trans couples, and there are a number of other resources out there. *Inviting Hera's Blessing* also contains a number of handfasting rites specifically for queer couples, and if you are planning an LGBT handfasting, you might want to check out some of Kaldera's ritual suggestions.

In this book, I do not go into the subject of poly handfastings, but there is no reason why you should not have a poly ceremony. I know several people who have undertaken one, and since pagans tend to be into alternative life-styles, quite a number are polyamorous and want to make a commitment to the people in their lives. In this case, you will need to make sure that the logistics of the ritual (for example, in the binding of hands) are clear to every-one, particularly your celebrant—you don't want your High Priestess getting in a muddle about multiple cord tying, for instance. As I was writing this sec-tion, my partner Trevor (who will be appearing throughout these pages) was negotiating with four women, who wanted to get handfasted in the same cer-emony. Not a problem—but we did need to work out the logistics and ask if we were handfasting two couples in the same ritual, or all four of them to each other.

In addition, it should be noted that you can have more than one or two celebrants. Although Trevor and I usually work as a team—High Priest and

High Priestess—you can involve more people if you wish. When I use the term *celebrant* in the text, remember that this can be plural as well as singular.

To use this book, you do not have to read it in a linear way from cover to cover. If there are particular aspects with which you are concerned (such as how to find a celebrant or what food to serve at your handfasting, or how to structure a ritual to the goddess Aphrodite), you can focus on those specific chapters and skip the history. If you want to combine a legally binding ceremony with a spiritual one, then chapter 2 will be of use to you. If you don't need a legal ceremony and just want a spiritual commitment, then you don't need to plough through the legal nitty-gritty.

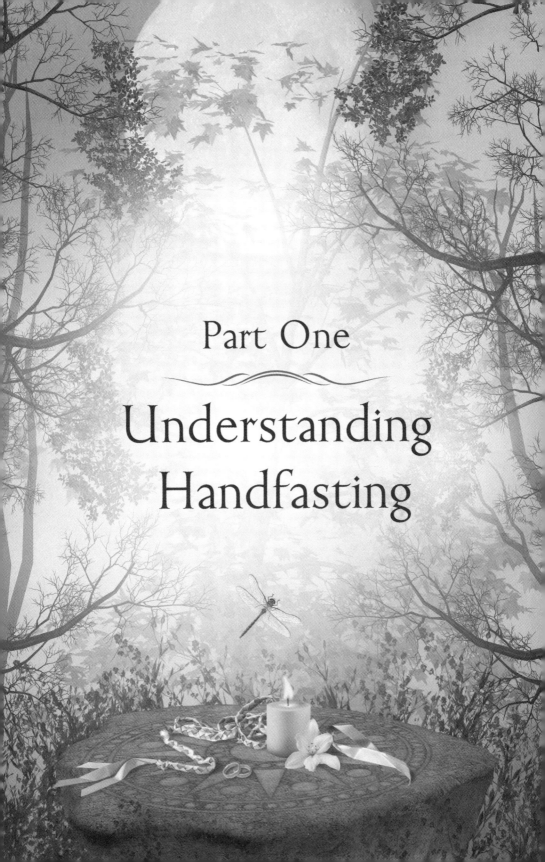

Part One

Understanding Handfasting

Chapter One
The History of Handfasting

Handfasting—the custom of marriage in modern paganism—is becoming increasingly popular. More mention of it is made in the mainstream media these days, and it is featured in wedding magazines. When I was in the process of completing this book, a wedding guide arrived through the letter box attached to the high-class British society magazine *The Tatler*. When I read it, I found that a large section of it was devoted specifically to handfastings—now becoming a popular form of ceremony among younger members of the aristocracy. Cressida Bonas, Prince Harry's ex, was quoted in it, talking about her battle with her dad, who wanted her to have a traditional church ceremony followed by a sit-down dinner and a speech. Bonas, however, said that her ideal choice of wedding location was "a tree," and judging by the Instagram evidence in which she and her new husband are literally riding off into a sunset woodland, she got her wish.

When did the custom of handfasting start? If you're familiar with expressions such as "jumping the broomstick" or "tying the knot," then you've already got a head start on what a handfasting might involve. For the sake of convenience, as celebrants, my partner Trevor and I tell people that handfasting is an ancient Celtic and Saxon rite—a marriage contract between the members of different tribes, which did not necessarily last forever. Suppose your tribe has been at loggerheads with the neighboring people for years. Everyone wants to sort this out. As chieftain, you arrange a handfasting between your son and the daughter of the rival chief. It only lasts for a year and a day—but that's enough time to cement the relationship between the two tribes, to make you all one family. Whether the relationship lasts or not, it doesn't matter; it's the initial ceremony and the thought behind it that count. Maybe the young couple will decide to make it a lifetime commitment. Maybe they'll part and get wed to their true loves after the year and a day are over. But they've brought the tribes together as one family, and that's what counts.

But is this narrative actually true? Where *did* the rite of handfasting begin? To answer this question, we'll take a look at some old texts that mention handfasting in the British Isles and see what kind of ceremonies they're talking about.

First, I should note that it's not strictly correct to describe handfasting as a "Celtic" rite. The term is first found in Late Old English, and it probably comes from Old Norse: *handfesta*, "to strike a bargain by joining hands." There are similar words in neighboring languages: Old Frisian has *hondfestinge*, while Middle Low German uses *hantvestinge*. Modern Dutch still uses the term—*handvest*—to mean the "making of a contract," and it has the same meaning in Middle to Early Modern English. It's actually the same as the Italian word *manifesto* (as in, *a political manifesto*), which comes from the Latin *manifestum*, meaning "clear" or "conspicuous." *Manifesto* is first found in English in the 1600s, so it's not a modern word even though it might sound like one.

The word *handfasting* itself turns up in documents from sixteenth- and seventeenth-century Scotland, and it specifically refers to a temporary marriage. The earliest mention, however, goes all the way back to 1200 and a text called the *Ormulum* manuscript—a work of biblical exegesis written by a monk named Orm or Ormin. This describes the Virgin Mary as "handfast" to a good man named Joseph:

> ჳho wass hanndfesst an god mann þatt iosæp wass ჳehatenn.[1]

---

1. Joseph R. Strayer, ed, "Ormulum," in *Dictionary of the Middle Ages* (New York: Charles Scribner's Sons, 1987), 1. 2389.

The term *handfasting* is genuinely old, and if you tell your relatives that it comes from the ancient British Isles and Northern Europe, you won't be misleading them!

What Are the Origins of Handfasting?

This is probably because of some of handfasting's Scottish roots. North of the border, from the twelfth to the seventeenth century, handfasting was a legal form of probationary marriage. It was an actual ceremony made in the presence of two adult witnesses. In the Hebrides, it was a trial marriage made for a year, during which the woman had to "please [her husband] all the while." (We don't necessarily write *that* bit into a modern ritual!)

Handfasting is referenced in Thomas Pennant's *Tour in Scotland*. This fascinating early travelogue is an account of Pennant's tour from Edinburgh to the Highlands, in which he comments on the botany and natural history of the country, as well as local customs and folklore. He tells us that,

> Among the various customs now obsolete the most curious was that of handfisting, in use about a century past. In the upper part of Eskdale … there was an annual fair where multitudes of each sex repaired. The unmarried looked out for mates, made their engagements by joining hands, or by handfisting, went off in pairs, cohabited until the next annual return of the fair, appeared there again and then were at liberty to declare their approbation or dislike of each other. If each party continued constant, the handfisting was renewed for life …[2]

Handfasting appears again in *The [Old] Statistical Account of Scotland*, which was commissioned by Sir John Sinclair, the Member of Parliament for Caithness, to give a picture of the political state of Scotland—but also, like Pennant's account, to include some of the social customs. The account refers to a piece of ground at the meeting point of the Esk Rivers and cites an annual fair, held there from ancient times, when unmarried men and women would choose a partner to live with for a year. It reads, "This was

2. Thomas Pennant, *Tour in Scotland* (London: B. White, 1776), 91.

called hand-fasting, or hand in fist. If they were pleased with each other at that time, then they continued together for life; if not, they separated, and were free to make another choice as at the first."[3] Any children would belong to the person who wanted to continue the relationship.

The account goes on to say that a priest, nicknamed a book i' bosom (probably because he carried either a bible or a marriage register in the bosom of his cassock), would come to the district in order to confirm these marriages.

This region is not far from the Roman encampment of Castle O'er, and some authorities have speculated that the handfasting fair might even date back to Roman times, perhaps as a holdover from the Roman form of marriage known as *ex usu* or *usus*. In this, a woman, if she had consent from her parents or guardians, would be allowed to live with a man for a year with no absences lasting longer than three nights. After this year-long period, she would be designated the man's wife.

Unfortunately, there are a few problems with these reports of handfasting history. First, Thomas Pennant is known for being fast and loose with his facts. He mentions that handfasting came about because of a shortage of the clergy, but marriage in Scotland wasn't actually dependent on having a cleric present. Second, the ceremony to which Pennant refers only appears in one small region of the Borders and might not apply to the whole of Scotland. Furthermore, the custom of *usus* was obsolete in Roman law by the time the Romans came as far as the Scottish borders, and, moreover, they never penetrated into Scotland itself (though it is possible that individual Roman families a little farther south might have kept the custom going).

Whatever the case, handfastings were banned in 1575 by the Kirk in Scotland and replaced by the sort of marriage ceremony with which we are familiar today. However, according to *The Scots Magazine*, records of the South Leith Church show that handfastings were being carried out thirty years after the ban; old customs die hard! Handfastings were still conducted in the Bor-

---

3. John Sinclair, *The [Old] Statistical Account of Scotland* (Edinburgh: William Creech, 1791–99), 617.

ders, and the place where the White Esk and Black Esk Rivers meet up near Bailiehill is called Handfasting Haugh. I think we can treat this as a clue.

Sir Walter Scott's character Avenel in his 1820 novel *The Monastery* says, "We Bordermen...take our wives, like our horses, upon trial. When we are handfasted, as we term it, we are man and wife for a year and a day: that space gone by, each may choose another mate, or at their pleasure, may call the priest to marry them for life—and this we call handfasting."[4]

Alexander Anton has done some thorough work on the history of handfasting in *Handfasting in Scotland* (which also quotes Pennant but notes that he wasn't altogether reliable as a scholar).[5] Anton also tells us that among people in the Lothians and Northumbria and in some of the Germanic tribes, marriages were performed in two stages. The betrothal ceremony (*beweddung* in Anglo-Saxon) came first, and after that, the wife was formally given away to her husband. In the *beweddung*, the husband gave "weds" or guarantees and sureties to his intended wife's relations, partly as a bride-price and partly as a dowry and wedding gift. The man and woman would shake hands to complete their contract, a process known as *handfæstung*.

The Dictionary of Older Scottish Tongue is an enormous, twelve-volume work which contains the history of the Scots language. The University of Dundee has digitized the whole thing—a mammoth task! The dictionary contains a sixteenth-century quote that reads as follows:

> ...the said dispensacione cum nocht hayme within the said tyme...the said John the Grant is bundin...to caus thame be handfast and put togiddir...for mariage to be completit; 1520 Grant Chart 64. Ib. 65. Because...many within this toun ar handfast, as thai call it, and maid promeis of mariage a lang space bygan...and as yit vill nocht mary

4. Walter Scott, *The Monastery* (Edinburgh: Constable and Ballantyne, 1820), 77.

5. Alexander Anton, *Handfasting in Scotland: The Scottish Historical Review* (Edinburgh, UK: Edinburgh University Press, 1958).

and coimpleit that honorable band…, but lyis and continewis in manifest fornicatioun…[6]

The Edinburgh Evening News, published in 1896, also tells us that the son of a chief would marry the daughter of another leader for a year and a day. If the wife gave birth to a son, the boy would inherit all rights; if not, the couple could part and were free to remarry. Marriage ceremonies contained an odd little wish: that the couple would experience "happy feet"! However, there's often a difference between historical accuracy and Victorian romanticism, so take this account with a grain of salt.

Handfasting marriages were also known in the official records as "contracted" marriages and, as we shall see elsewhere, may have been regarded more as an engagement or betrothal. An article in *The Scots Magazine* says, "There can be little doubt, however, that in too many cases, the mere betrothal was looked upon by parties as an actual marriage. In 1575—15 years after the Reformation—the General Assembly evidently desired to put a stop to this evil."[7] The Kirk insisted that if you wanted to be wed properly, you should give your name so that your banns could be proclaimed. In Aberdeen, it was ordered "that neither the minister nor reader be present at contractis of their marriage, making as thai call thair handfasting…"[8]

The custom is also mentioned by Martin Martin in the 1600s, who wrote about the Western Isles of Scotland and the Isle of Man. Martin wrote, "It was an ancient custom in the Isles that a man take a maid as his wife and keep her for the space of a year without marrying her; and if she pleased him all the while, he married her at the end of the year and legitimatized her children; but if he did not love her, he returned her to her parents."[9]

---

6. William Craigie, *The Dictionary of Older Scottish Tongue* (Dundee: University of Dundee, 1931–2002), 65.

7. *The Scots Magazine* (Dundee: University of Dundee, 1933).

8. Newsroom, "The origins of handfasting at Scottish weddings—When Scots 'married' for a year and a day," *Scotsman*, accessed November 3, 2020, https://www.scotsman.com/regions/origins-handfasting-scottish-weddings-when-scots-married-year-and-day-113813.

9. Martin Martin, *A Description of the Western Islands of Scotland* (Cornhil: A. Bell, 1776).

In this case, the year-long period is basically a kind of trial marriage: the couple would be expected to sleep together and have children, and it appears that the marriage would then be legitimized on the man's say-so at the end of the term.

There has been a suggestion that the handfasting ceremony comes from the Viking history of the Isle of Man, but historians tend to disagree, pointing out that Viking engagements could indeed be quite long, but there is no evidence of this "year and a day" practice. In fact, handfastings seem to have been more a kind of civil ceremony that could only be broken by death, divorce not being a possibility in those days. The English legal authorities regarded handfasting—which the Jacobeans and Elizabethans termed a "troth plight"—as being as legally binding as marriage itself and a lot more formal than a trial marriage (a "troth plight" is when a couple "plight"—make—the "troth"—a promise—to one another). There seem to have been different forms of handfasting, at various levels of formality and legality, at different times, around the country. Although of historical interest to our inquiry, these varying forms don't really impact whatever we choose to undertake in terms of a handfasting ceremony today.

Handfastings and Engagements

Ecclesiastical law covered two kinds of handfasting and presented them essentially as a form of engagement:

Sponsalia per verba de praesenti (betrothal by words at the present time): The couple accepts one another as man and wife.

Sponsalia per verba de futuro: The couple declares their intention to marry each other at some future date. This can be ended with the consent of both parties, but only if they haven't had sex. If they have, then the *sponsalia de futuro* is converted into *de iure* marriage.

This form of engagement was supposed to be converted into a church wedding in due course, otherwise there were penalties to pay. In addition, you were supposed to abstain from sex (although human nature being what it is, clerics complained that people often didn't).

In Pollock and Maitland's *History of English Law*, the authors state that handfasting "established a bond which could not be dissolved except under exceptional circumstances, and not at all if copula carnalis had taken place."[10] Calvinist preacher Heinrich Bullinger emphasizes the point:

> After the handfasting & making of the contract, the churchgoing & wedding should not be deferred too long, lest the wicked sew his ungracious seed in the mean season.[11]

Shakespeare and Love

An example of a *sponsalia per verba* crops up in the life of Shakespeare. The playwright was a guest at a handfasting in 1604 and acted as a witness (imagine having Shakespeare at your wedding!). He was living on Silver Street in London at the time, where the handfasting took place. The Mountjoys, parents of the bride, were his landlord and landlady. Daniel Nichols, who was also present and a friend of both Shakespeare and the couple, describes the type of ceremony as follows: "In matrimonie there is a contract or makyng sure, there is a coupling or handfasting of eyther partie, and finally marriage."[12]

The couple, Stephen Belott and Mary Mountjoy, said that Nichols "agreed to marry, giving each other's hand to the hand, and did marry."[13] Some historians have speculated that his own marriage to Anne Hathaway might also have taken the form of a handfasting.

10. Frederick Pollock and Frederic Maitland, *History of English Law* (Indianapolis: Liberty Fund, 2010).

11. Charles Nicholl, "The Lodger Shakespeare: His Life on Silver Street," *Erenow*, accessed November 3, 2020, https://erenow.net/biographies/the-lodger-shakespeare-his-life-on-silver-street.

12. Nicholl, "The Lodger Shakespeare."

13. Nicholl, "The Lodger Shakespeare."

Shakespeare wasn't the only poet of the day to take part in this kind of ritual. In 1601, the metaphysical writer John Donne took part in a clandestine marriage in a private room. Donne himself, his bride, his friend Christopher Brooke, and Brooke's brother Samuel, who was a clergyman, were the only people present. They did not call the banns, and the bride's parents had not given consent, but the validity of the marriage was not subsequently disputed by the bride's father.

Elsewhere, Henry Swinburne, a judge at the Prerogative Court in York, wrote in his work *Treatise of Spousals* that those who "have contracted spousals de praesenti are reputed man and wife…For spousals de praesenti, though not consummate, be in truth and substance very matrimony.[14] Thus we can see that this form of marriage was regarded as legitimate, even if the marriage was not consummated.

Shakespeare and Swinburne are not the only people to be referenced in regard to handfastings. In John Webster's famous play *The Duchess of Malfi*, we find the following:

> I have heard lawyers say a contract in a chamber
>
> > Per verba presenti is absolute marriage.
>
> Bless, heaven, this sacred gordian which let violence
>
> > Never untwine!…
>
> How can the church build faster?
>
> We are now man and wife, and 'tis the church
>
> That must but echo this.[15]

The message coming from these accounts is that handfastings were regarded at the time as legitimate and legal forms of marriage. Handfastings also seem to have been relatively common.

---

14. Henry Swinburne, *Treatise of Spousals* (London: Daniel Brown, Thomas Ward, and William Mears, 1711).

15. John Webster, *The Duchess of Malfi* (London: Okes, 1612–13), 1.2.18–35.

"She Knew What She Did"

William Addison, in a case before the London Consistory Court around 1610, is recorded as telling the bride, Joan Waters, "to take heed what she did … for it was a contract that was not for a day or a month but for term of life, and Joan answered she knew what she did."[16] This is pretty explicit in that handfasting is not supposed to be for a year and a day alone, but is a serious lifetime commitment.

The Consistory Court has records of a number of disputed marriage cases, in which a number of troth plights are mentioned. They take place in a wide variety of locations, such as the local pub, the bride's home (a popular choice), in an orchard, and even on horseback.

The words of these troth plights will be familiar to us as there are echoes of the marriage ceremony today. Take the following vows in this 1598 handfasting officiated by John Griffin: "'I John take thee Jane to my wedded wife, till death us depart, and thereto I plight thee my troth'; and then the woman to say the like words again. This, Griffin said, do make folks sure together."[17]

When a couple named Thomas and Grace were married, Thomas took his bride by the hand and said, "I Thomas take thee Grace to my wife, and I will have thee to my wife and no other woman, and thereto I plight thee my troth." "And then they loosing hands, Grace took Thomas by the right hand, saying: I Grace take thee Thomas to my husband [etc] …"[18]

In the case of another couple, Elizabeth took Martin by the hand "and said unto him these very words and none other: 'Here is my hand, in faith forever, whether my mother will or no.' And then the said Martin answered: 'There is my hand and my faith forever, and I will never forsake thee.'"[19] One has to wonder if Elizabeth's mother had raised an objection!

The 1753 Marriage Act regularized wedding ceremonies, however, and handfastings and troth plights fell out of favor from that point onward. From then on, marriage ceremonies were closer in form to our modern wedding

16. Nicholl, "The Lodger Shakespeare."

17. Nicholl, "The Lodger Shakespeare."

18. Nicholl, "The Lodger Shakespeare."

19. Nicholl, "The Lodger Shakespeare."

ceremonies in English-speaking countries, but we can see in some of the examples above echoes of the words that are still familiar to us today.

Handfasting in Ireland

I've looked at England and Scotland, but what was the situation over the sea in Ireland? Fortunately, we know a lot about Irish medieval law: it's well documented. Known as Brehon Law, its texts give details of statutes concerning life in early medieval Ireland. Brehon Law was subsumed by the Norman Conquest in 1169, but was then revived from the thirteenth to seventeenth century and lasted into Early Modern Ireland in parallel with English law. Brehon Law is a civil code rather than a criminal code. It's comprehensive, giving a window into the importance of social status in the hierarchical society of Ireland, and it places a strong emphasis on compensation. It is heavily concerned with contract, and since marriage of various forms is a kind of contract, we find this outlined in some detail within Brehon Law.

For enlightenment on how the Irish celebrated marriage, our first stop is the *Cáin Lánamna*: the Law of Couples. This is an Old Irish text dated to circa 700 AD and is one of the primary sources of information concerning the role of women and the household economy in early Ireland. The *Cáin Lánamna* describes every form of recognized marriages and unions, legal and illegal, and details the allocation of property in the event of a divorce.[20] It deals with various kinds of marriage, including ordinary unions between couples, but it also has legal provision for marriages that were carried out through abduction, or between wandering mercenaries, or even through rape. This was a legal code which covered as many possibilities as it could. Interestingly, there is also some provision in Brehon Law for polygamy. What Irish law does not cover, however, is the length of time that a union should last. It would seem that Irish law, too, does not cover this "year and a day" concept.

Handfasting in Modern Times

After handfasting, troth plights, and all the other various forms of marriage became obsolete or outlawed and were replaced by the legal marriage ceremony

---

20. Charlene Eska, *Cáin Lánamna: An Old Irish Tract on Marriage and Divorce Law* (Leiden: Brill, 2009).

that is more familiar to us today, handfastings do not appear in literature again as contemporary ceremonies until the twentieth century. With the rise of Wicca and modern witchcraft, plus other forms of pagan paths, handfastings were once more adopted—this time as a pagan ceremony.

In the historical examples I've given above, all of these handfastings would have been Christian in spirit: paganism did not, despite claims to the contrary, survive in any ancient form in Britain after the Norman conquest at the very latest, although witchcraft and magical practice did. The handfasting ceremony that Shakespeare attended would have cited the Christian God or Christ, if indeed it mentioned anything. It is not until Gerald Gardner established Wicca in Southern England that handfasting was adopted by pagans and once more became popular as an alternative to marriage. Pagan authors such as Stewart and Janet Farrar included sample handfasting ceremonies in books such as *The Witch's Bible*. Nowadays, handfastings are a common and popular form of union—not only between pagan couples, as we shall see in the pages to follow, but among others, too.

Conclusion

We know that although handfasting might have ancient roots, it is not itself a very old form of union—it is a few hundred years old, rather than thousands. However, it is not misleading, if you are a celebrant, to tell your handfastees that the custom has its origins in the British Isles and Northern Europe. They've come for a wedding, not a history lecture. That said, it's important that, as a celebrant, you understand the origins of what you are doing. And it's nice for both handfastees and celebrants to be able to inform people properly about the ceremony if they show an interest.

Chapter Two
The Legality of Handfasting

Are handfastings legal? As I alluded to in the beginning of this book, the answer to this question is both *yes* and *no*. The legality of your handfasting will depend on your location: which country or state you reside in. I ought to stress that by "legal," I don't mean that it is *illegal* to conduct a handfasting, simply that in some places, the marriage won't be binding under law. Don't worry—you won't be arrested!

In some countries or states, handfastings can be legally binding. It all depends on the law in your particular location. In some regions, you will need to have both a handfasting and a legally binding wedding ceremony (for example, at a registrar's office) at separate times. In others, the handfasting and the legal service can be bound into one ceremony. You must discuss this with your celebrant, especially if you want to have a legally binding marriage. In this chapter, we will take a look at the law in some specific countries: those Western nations that probably have the highest concentration of those who follow modern pagan paths.

Celebrant Helen Woodsford-Dean undertakes handfastings with her partner, Mark, in the beautiful and ancient islands of the Orkneys, in the North of Scotland. Helen has been handfasting couples for many years and is particularly knowledgeable about the legal aspects of handfasting in Scotland.

She carries out other ceremonies and celebrations, too, and has recently been instrumental in setting up a memorial to all those who died in the witch trials in the area.

Helen counsels,

Legal weddings bring their own issues, and we now specifically state that we won't go ahead if they cannot produce a schedule (like a marriage license) or are too drunk or don't understand English sufficiently. Since we can go to prison if we break this, we think we are allowed to be stricter about this. However, our permissions to perform fully legal weddings comes via the Scottish Pagan Federation, so we do include pagan traditions in these ceremonies—using words that honor nature, perhaps a handfasting, or jumping of the broomstick—all of which are traditions steeped in time.

Make sure that you and your celebrant know the law in your particular area, as legislation can vary widely. German celebrant Cat Pentaberry says, for example, that "in Germany … any kind of religious ceremony must come after the state sanctioned one."

In short, make sure you know the law—and be aware that the law can change, too. The legislation regarding handfasting has altered over the last few decades in part of the British Isles, Ireland, and the US, for example.

Now, we will look at the legislation across a range of countries.

United States of America

Handfastings are legally binding in all fifty states if the celebrant is registered by the individual state in question to perform wedding ceremonies and you get a marriage license and follow the relevant laws of the state.

In 2015, the US Supreme Court ruled that same-sex marriage is a legal right across the United States. You will need to consult the law of your state to check if your handfasting ceremony is legally binding—the same laws should apply as to heterosexual couples, but it is wise to double-check.

If you are interested in being handfasted in the US: Check with local pagan groups, pagan bookstores, or the authorities in your particular state.

How to become a celebrant in the US: There are a number of organizations, such as the Celebrant Foundation and Institute, in the States that provide training and certification for aspiring celebrants. The Troth, Covenant of the Goddess, and Circle Sanctuary are also big US-based national organizations that can recommend celebrants and also offer credentials to legally marry people. Check which one might be suitable for you and whether the course gives you full powers to marry people legally.

Australia

Handfasting is legal in Australia provided that a licensed marriage celebrant conducts your ceremony.

Same-sex marriage has been legal in the country since 2017; if you are engaging in an LGBT handfasting performed by a licensed celebrant, the ceremony should be legal, but it is sensible to double-check this with your state's legislation.

If you are interested in being handfasted in Australia: Contact the Attorney General's Office if you are seeking a licensed pagan celebrant.

How to become a celebrant in Australia: In order to be able to legally marry people in Australia, you will need to be an authorized marriage celebrant. To register as a Commonwealth marriage celebrant, you must have any of the following:

- A Certificate IV in Celebrancy from a registered training organization (RTO)
- A qualification in celebrancy
- Skills in celebrancy

Canada

A number of government functions in Canada fall under a provincial remit. Thus, each province has a different legal act when it comes to marriage, specifying which religious denominations may hold a legally binding wedding, or which denominations may appoint a legal celebrant. For instance, in Ontario, pagan organizations are not permitted to carry out legal handfastings, but celebrants are allowed to do so through a for-profit organization: All Seasons Weddings. In British Colombia, the CWA (Congregationalist Wiccan Association) has a number of celebrants.

Same-sex marriages have been legally recognized across Canada since July 2005, so if your celebrant is allowed to solemnize the marriage itself and you are a same-sex couple, you will be legally married.

If you are interested in being handfasted in Canada: As noted above, this will depend on your state, so contact the relevant organizations. They should also be able to put you in touch with the relevant celebrants elsewhere in Canada.

How to become a celebrant in Canada: In order to conduct legal weddings in Canada, you will need to become a licensed officiant. This is a secular post and is licensed by each province. If you are, for example, licensed by Ontario, you will be able to perform weddings in that province, but you will need to apply for a separate license for different provinces.

England and Wales

England and Wales are behind Ireland and Scotland in that handfastings do not yet, as a general rule, have legal status, despite a number of petitions. While it is legal to conduct a handfasting, the ceremony does not confer a legal status upon its participants. Nor can you combine your civil legal ceremony with a handfasting at the same time, as you are not legally permitted to have a legally binding civil ceremony with any religious content.

This applies whether you are a male-female or same-sex couple. If you are LGBT, you can marry legally in England, but not in a handfasting ceremony. As with other couples, you will need two separate ceremonies if you wish your union to be legally binding.

The plus side of this is that anyone can act as a celebrant without having to sign up as a registrar; the downside is that you need to have two separate ceremonies.

I said above, "as a general rule," there is at least one exception: the Goddess Temple in Glastonbury. Marriage in Scotland is connected to the person doing the ceremony—for example, to the registrar—whereas in England and Wales, the status of the building is also crucial. Therefore, Christian priests or ministers are only allowed to perform legal marriages in their own churches; their name is tied into a specific licensed religious location. Priestess Dawn Kinsella spearheaded this change, having obtained signatures from forty local people to confirm that the Temple is indeed a local place of worship. It is now permitted to hold legal handfastings there, including same-sex handfastings.

Hopefully, other places will be allowed to follow suit, and eventually handfastings will be made legal in England and Wales.

If you are interested in being handfasted in England and Wales: Speak to the Pagan Federation or contact the Goddess Temple directly, or arrange your own ceremony by speaking to a private celebrant.

How to become a celebrant in England and Wales: See notes for Scotland about the NOCN Level 3 Diploma in Celebrancy: Naming and Couples (RQF).

Ireland

Due to tireless campaigning by the Pagan Federation of Ireland and the work of Ray Sweeney, National Coordinator of the Pagan Federation International (PFI), handfasting was declared legal in Ireland some years ago, despite sustained opposition. Sweeney, speaking to the Pagan Federation in 2013, said that he "fought for it with the tenacity of a cornered rat."[21]

The law here was changed via protests, ministerial appeals, and equality tribunals and was part of a governmental review of marriage legislation in

---

21. Ray Sweeney, "Pagan Federation of Ireland—the Ray Sweeney interview," *Languageofmoons*, accessed November 3, 2020, https://languageofmoons.wordpress.com/2010/06/20/pagan-federation-of-ireland-the-ray-sweeney-interview/.

general in the form of a prelegislative submission on marriage recognition for nonmainstream religious couples. The PFI contributed to this in the draft stages.

LGBT people were not included in this legislation but can undertake civil partnerships. If you are part of an LGBT couple, your handfasting will not be legal in Ireland, and you will need to take part in a civil partnership ceremony with a separate handfasting. Sweeney says, "Our original submission was largely to the effect that any group, who shared common religious beliefs, and could prove a need by having more than 1,000 adherents, should be entitled to nominate a legal Solemniser from within their group. This would enable a couple to be married in a personally meaningful religious manner, by a member of their peer group."[22]

The law states that the religious ceremony of any authorized religious body (in this case, the PFI) is the concern of the religious body alone, once certain legal declarations are included.

If you are interested in being handfasted in Ireland: Contact the PFI and the Registrar of Marriages.

How to become a celebrant in Ireland: Contact the PFI, the Humanist Association of Ireland, or the Irish Institute of Celebrants, which offers professional training to people who want to become celebrants, either as online training or as an in-person course.

New Zealand

Handfasting can be legally binding in New Zealand, but you will need to apply for a marriage license. Same-sex marriage in New Zealand has been legal since August 19, 2013.

If you are interested in being handfasted in New Zealand: Contact your local registry office and find out if they have a list of handfasting celebrants or check online.

---

22. Sweeney, "Pagan Federation of Ireland."

How to become a celebrant in New Zealand: Independent celebrants can legally perform marriages and civil unions in New Zealand. You can be a marriage celebrant or a civil union celebrant or both. An application to become an independent celebrant costs two hundred twenty dollars.

Scotland

Under the Marriage (Scotland) Act 1977, it is now legal to have a legally binding handfasting. In 2004, handfastings became recognized under law in Scotland, again with the aid of the Pagan Federation of Scotland. Their celebrants gained authorization from the General Register Office for Scotland to perform legal weddings.

This law includes LGBT couples. You can have a legally binding same-sex handfasting in Scotland. In addition, if you come from another country that recognizes same-sex marriages, your ceremony will be legally binding in your own country if you are handfasted in Scotland. Helen Woodsford-Dean, whom we met earlier in this chapter, says,

We made inquiries [when planning our own handfasting] and discovered that Scottish law is different and that sites do not need to be licensed for weddings; the permissions go with the registrar, minister, or celebrant performing the ceremony.

Being Pagans ourselves, once based in Orkney, we were approached by the Scottish Pagan Federation about becoming celebrants. By 2010, we had completed the checking and registration processes and were performing our first weddings.

We have trained with the Fellowship of Professional Celebrants and with the Order of Bards, Ovates & Druids. We call ourselves "Spiritual Orkney," and we design and perform ceremonies to celebrate handfastings, engagements, betrothals, fully legal weddings, anniversaries, baby namings, family blessings, renewals of vows, and, of course, memorials.

If you are interested in being handfasted in Scotland: Contact the Pagan Federation (Scotland).

How to become a celebrant in Scotland: If you are interested in becoming a qualified celebrant in Scotland, England, or Wales, there is a national diploma: the NOCN Level 3 Diploma in Celebrancy: Naming and Couples (RQF). This diploma is the highest-level accredited national qualification available in Naming and Couples Celebrancy in the UK. Within paganism, many celebrants are not formally qualified, but they are members of covens, Druidic groves, and so on, who have been asked to perform handfastings and continue to do so. Although the ceremony will not be binding under law, it is perfectly legal.

Conclusion

In this chapter, we have seen that the law on handfasting varies widely from country to country—and in some nations, from state to state. In some countries, it can be legally binding, but in others, it is not, and you will need to have a separate ceremony if you want a legally binding marriage. It is advisable, therefore, that you look into the law in your own region and/or the region in which you are planning to have your handfasting. If in doubt, check with your local law practice or pagan organization. They will be happy to advise you, and you can discuss it with your celebrant, too.

Chapter Three

Things to Consider

Having considered the history and legality of the ceremony, we'll now be looking at how to organize a handfasting. I'll cover how to find a celebrant, your choice of location, photography, and whether to have an exchange of rings, tie hands together, or jump the broomstick. These are all questions you will be asking if you have not had a handfasting before; sometimes the logistics can seem daunting, and you may feel that you don't know how to proceed.

I'll start from the very beginning, therefore, and assume that this is the first time you're having a handfasting. What is your starting point once you've decided to undertake this kind of ceremony? We'll begin with some initial thoughts and questions.

Questions to Ask Yourself

After the first excitement of realizing that you want a ceremony that binds your lives together, whether it's a handfasting or a legal wedding ceremony (or both), there are some things you need to think about, both practical and spiritual.

Remember, it is a good idea to start thinking about your ceremony a year or so in advance. Many venues are booked up in the longer term, and your celebrants may not be able to attend at the drop of a hat, either. It's a lot less stressful to arrange your handfasting well in advance.

Why Do You Specifically Want a Handfasting?

Do you want a handfasting just because it sounds like an appealing ceremony (it's fine if you do)? Or are there deeper spiritual reasons for your choice? Do you follow a particular pagan path or a specific god, goddess, or pantheon? Whatever the case, just as with any marriage ceremony, it's a good idea to work out the reasons why you're going into this commitment, whether you decide to follow the "year and a day" principle or sign up for the rest of your lives.

Paul Cudby is a Church of England vicar—it may surprise you to learn that we consulted a Christian priest with reference to a book about a pagan ceremony! However, Paul incorporates elements of handfasting in wedding ceremonies conducted in a church, such as the binding of hands. He is also involved in Forest Church, a movement that encourages Christians to go out into nature and experience the magic of the natural world within their own religious ceremonies. We asked him for his views on the spiritual side of marriage, and this is what he had to say:

I consider it to be a deep privilege and a sharing in a mystery. Reflecting on this from the perspective of a Church of England priest who binds hands together as a part of the marriage ceremony, I have lost track of the number of couples, many who have been together for a long while and some with children in tow, who have told me at some point after the service that something changed in their relationship. I look at this as how a sacrament is an outward and visible sign of an inward grace, and so my binding of their hands together is a visible symbol of the work the Spirit has done in binding their souls together. This, however, is only the beginning. They must work together to deepen that bond. Some couples reflect on how, after decades together, they are unsure where they stop and their partner starts. This, in itself, is reflective of the bond between disciple and God, that sometimes thoughts, feelings, and prayers well up within, and we don't know whether it is the self who is thinking or the Spirit within.

With regard to his own marriage blessing, Paul adds,

Reflecting on our twenty-fifth anniversary celebrations conducted in a grove by Reverend Simon Marshall, another earth-focused priest, [we decided that] the priority was to be located in a place that resonated with us, surrounded by those who love us, and to celebrate the lifelong commitment to which we have pledged ourselves. In a sense, because we had already made sacramental vows, the unseen binding of souls had begun twenty-five years previously. This was a celebration and a declaration of how deeply those bonds had penetrated and changed us. It was also a creative expression of who we were in 2014 compared to who we were in 1989.

It is always a good idea to talk your thoughts through with your celebrant. Some people are a bit embarrassed to admit that they're not actually pagan—but your celebrant won't necessarily expect you to be! A professional celebrant should never make assumptions, and most have been approached by people from all religions (or none) who want this particular form of ceremony for a wide variety of reasons. Some handfasting couples, even if they are pagan, might not be quite sure what they want, and a good celebrant will be able to give them some suggestions.

Helen Woodsford-Dean adds her own take on the matter:

For couples: Think about the ceremonies you have been to. What did you like? What didn't you like? Find a celebrant who is sincere and genuine, who is willing to be flexible. Listen to what you want, but also make appropriate suggestions for things that will suit you when you have run out of ideas. [You will need a celebrant] with enough experience to know the potential problems of any site, time, and so on, [w]ho will anticipate, who will go the extra mile, and who enjoys what they do with a passion. And trust your celebrant to know what they are doing.

Paul also gave us some further thoughts:

Take it very seriously and recognize that the handfasting is outwardly symbolic of a potential real change in the soul. Look for it and embrace it, but recognize it requires self-sacrifice and commitment to make it work. It must always be about giving and never about taking. For the celebrant, that truth requires of us that we take the responsibility very seriously.

Finding a Celebrant

The person who conducts your handfasting is obviously really important. We can't have Shakespeare at our wedding! But where can you find a celebrant?

Where you look for a celebrant will depend on the following:

- Are you seeking a purely legal ceremony? (In which case, you may not need a pagan celebrant specifically and will need to contact your local registrar or other individual who is licensed to conduct a legal ceremony.)
- Are you seeking a religious ceremony?
- The path you are currently following (and it might be no path at all as of yet) or the tradition you are in.

I have conducted handfastings for people who are not pagans, and this is by no means uncommon. Perhaps they like the nature-based atmosphere of pagan ceremonies and the idea of holding their celebration in a beautiful natural landscape. They may come from different religious traditions and seek to find a compromise within paganism (to date, I have handfasted a couple who were Hindu and atheist, and I have also conducted a handfasting for a Catholic whose legal wife was refusing him a divorce on religious grounds).

If you are on a pagan path, whether Wiccan, Druid, Heathen, or other, you may want your presiding priest or priestess to conduct the ceremony, and they will probably be delighted to do so. You might also want someone else from your ritual working group to perform the nuptials—perhaps a close friend, for example.

If, however, your High Priest(ess) is unavailable for any reason, or if you are of a solitary persuasion and are not plugged into any particular tradition, or you're not pagan at all and just want the ceremony itself, you have a number of options when it comes to finding a celebrant:

- Word of mouth and personal recommendations.
- An online search (in this case, check whether the person is a professional celebrant, whether they have any recommendations from satisfied handfastees, what they will provide, and what they charge).

- Esoteric stores (they may have details of local celebrants, and many people who run witchcraft or occult shops undertake handfastings themselves).
- Contacting an organization, such as the Pagan Federation or Life Rites in the UK, or the Troth, Covenant of the Goddess, and Circle Sanctuary in the US.
- Asking a friend (this can be lovely, but make sure they actually know what they're doing!).
- DIY. There is no reason why you shouldn't handfast yourselves. My partner and I did so at Chalice Well in Glastonbury very early one winter solstice morning, and it was a beautiful experience.

What Should I Look for in a Celebrant?

If at all possible, meet your celebrant before the handfasting—and preferably some time before, not on the eve of the ceremony. Most of our handfastees set up an appointment a year or so before their big day, and this is wise; these events can take a long time to plan. Popular celebrants, just like vicars and clergy from other religions, can be booked up a long time in advance, and so can venues. Most people do have a good idea of the time frame, but some folk really don't—and expect miracles in a couple of weeks.

It is crucial to have your ceremony conducted by someone you like and whom you trust. This is one of the most important rituals of your life, and if you don't get on with someone or if you feel uneasy around them, then don't have any qualms about letting them know (in good time, courteously, and in writing, if necessary) that you've found someone else. If they're professionals, they won't mind.

Consider the following points when forming a relationship with a prospective celebrant:

- Make sure they have your full contact details.
- Check that they are clear about the names you will be using in the ceremony (some people use their pagan name rather than their birth name). Celebrants have a horror of getting a name wrong, so make sure that this is clear.

- Make sure that your celebrant is clear, too, about the time and date of the ceremony. They should drop you an email, a call, or a text in the weeks leading up to the handfasting to check that it's still going ahead (and I always contact handfastees the day before, as well). Not hearing from a celebrant until the night before the handfasting—or even the morning of the service!—is enough to make anyone jittery.
- Your celebrant should discuss with you the full format of the ceremony and send you a copy of it. Some people want a long and elaborate handfasting with room for songs, speeches, and poems, and some people really just want the opportunity to say their basic vows.
- Your celebrant should check the numbers with you—conducting a big handfasting is different from conducting a small and intimate ceremony consisting of just you and your partner.
- Your celebrant may want, roughly, the ages of participants. In some locations, it's not possible for people to sit down, and if you are planning to invite older relatives or friends or people with disabilities, this should make your celebrant start asking questions about the length of the handfasting, as some people may not be able to stand for long periods of time.
- Your celebrant should also guide you through the vows. Experienced celebrants can suggest formats for vows, how to write them, what to say, and so forth. If I have one piece of advice to give to handfastees after thirty years of conducting rituals, it is this: **write your vows down.** You think you'll remember them. You might not! (I will give some advice about writing your vows in a later chapter).
- Your celebrant should also check which gods/goddesses/spirits you want to address in your ceremony. I often have handfastees who work with a patron deity—such as Rhiannon, Gwyn ap Neath, Venus, or the Green Man—and who want a reference to that deity during the course of the handfasting.

I spoke to Helen Johnson of UK-based celebrancy organization Life Rites about her approach to handfastings. Helen is an experienced celebrant and has done extensive training in organizing ceremonies of different kinds. Life Rites is based on the South Coast of England and is a not-for-profit organization, arranging ceremonies of many different kinds, from handfastings to coming-of-age ceremonies and eldership rites. Helen tells us how she initiates a handfasting ceremony:

I approach a handfasting with a clear and open mind. I find out if the couple have a specific branch of paganism or Wicca or whether it is a symbolic hand-fasting—when I first started as a celebrant, I made the mistake of assuming that a couple were Wiccan, and they were not; they had merely read about the idea and were somewhat bemused by my goddess referencing.

In either case, I take a bit of time during the initial meeting to discuss what handfasting means to me, to the couple, and in a wider sphere socially, spiritually, and culturally. I ask if specific deities are to be invoked and what type of altar the couple would like. If it is a mixed-faith (even within pagan-ism) ceremony, I ask how they would prefer their deity to be symbolized, rep-resented, and worked with.

I have three generic handfasting ceremonies prepared, which I will have emailed to the couple to peruse before the meeting (simple, more involved, and pretty complex), and hopefully they will have decided which they favor. I gen-erally discuss with the couple the possibility that not all their guests may be aware of what a handfasting is, and some may not be comfortable with it. I encourage them to explain to people what handfasting means to them.

As with any ceremony, I will make many notes, ask open-ended questions, and attempt to glean as much information as possible. (Sometimes the simple ceremony works well with those guests not as comfortable with the notion of handfasting.) I encourage the couple to write their own vows separately and not to show the vows to their partner prior to the ceremony (they send them to me, and I can, of course, assist).

At the end of the initial meeting, I talk to them about the actual binding ribbons, asking whether they want to have them made (I can provide contacts) or to create their own individual cords themselves (which I favor, as these are much more personal, magical, and, I feel, powerful for the binding). I will then spend time researching and trying some ritual meditation with each of their deities. We discuss what they want me to wear, if there is a theme, and so on. I send drafts of the ceremonies, and we work with everything and everybody who is participating in a key role (sometimes other people are ribbon bearers, there are musicians and various readings, etc.). I do this until we are all satisfied.

I generally have a second meeting to encourage them to create their vows and the handfasting ribbons. Before the ceremony, there is a dress rehearsal, and we work out which type of knot to use when tying (drape, wrap, release and pull, side by side … there are multiple options) and allow the couple a few attempts. I try to have a bath in purifying oils and salt before the ceremony, and I bless the area where the ceremony is taking place prior to guests and the couple arriving. During the ceremony, prior to tying the knot, I bless the ribbons.

What Will You Need to Bring to the Ceremony?

You also need to think about what you need to bring to the ceremony, and what will be supplied by the celebrant.

- Are you going to be bringing your own handfasting cord, or do you want the celebrant to supply this?
- Are you planning to jump a broomstick, and will you bring this yourself, or do you want the celebrant to supply this as well?
- Are there any other accessories that you are intending to bring? Do you want to use your own ritual tools, or would you rather that the celebrant uses their own? (I will look at ritual tools in a later chapter.)

Remember, the great thing about a handfasting is its flexibility. You can take as much or as little control over the ceremony as you wish, and an experienced celebrant should respect your wishes. Don't let a celebrant ride roughshod over your plans and intentions or impose a ritual structure on you. Guidelines are fine, but make sure that your prospective celebrant runs through the ceremony with you first. You have the right of refusal!

Do You Have a Budget for Your Celebrant?

This is obviously a big question, if a rather unromantic one. Budgeting can be a problem, because paganism doesn't tend to have central regulatory authorities—unlike the Christian Church—and thus it doesn't have fixed costs, either. Fortunately, most celebrants whom I have come across are professional in behavior, even if they aren't licensed, and they don't overcharge.

Celebrants in the UK tend to "peg" their costs to the rates charged by Christian vicars—about two hundred pounds per ceremony. This is the rate I charge, and I also charge basic travel expenses if I have to drive out of our county of Somerset. It's a good idea to choose a celebrant with a driving license; not every pagan location is easy to reach by public transport.

Pagan celebrants in the US say that they have done handfastings for a twenty-five-dollar donation, but they have also charged up to three hundred fifty dollars (plus travel expenses) for more distant events that may take more of their time. The cost will depend on what is involved.

If you're not happy with the amount suggested by a celebrant—and they do vary—then shop around. No one should be charging thousands of pounds or dollars to conduct a handfasting, and you don't want to be ripped off. If you're not a pagan (or even if you are!), be careful not to be impressed by someone's claims about being a "big name." Paganism is not yet one of the main world religions, and anyone you approach will be a big fish in a small pond, nothing more. Paganism, thankfully, is not known for having resident gurus, and neither should it have; some people may have spent a longer amount of time following their path and be more experienced, but we are all spiritually equal.

Some modern pagans believe that handfastings should not be paid for in cash, but in barter. There are a number of traditions that take the view that you should never charge money for magic or ritual, which is fair enough, but other pagans hold that if you are providing a service, it is fair to charge a fee for that service. Both are viable viewpoints.

Your Guests and Who You Invite

Some people want everyone to come to their handfasting. Some people prefer as few people as possible! A lot of this is going to depend on whether or not your family and friends are pagan themselves, and how sympathetic they are to your own beliefs.

Cat Pentaberry is a German celebrant and an old friend of ours. As well as having had a handfasting herself, she arranges handfasting ceremonies for other people and has a lot of experience in what can go wrong—and right! Cat says, "Don't invite people you just want to impress... It's a very personal commitment, and you will feel happiest when the people you share it with are real friends, pagan or not. I'd say this is not the moment to proselytize or showcase one's beliefs."

What If Your Guests Are Not Pagan?

This can obviously be a thorny issue, and I'll be looking at it in more detail later on. Sometimes relatives disinvite themselves: this usually happens if you have a relative who, for example, is a fundamentalist Christian and wants to make a point. It's sad, but it's really their loss. It's up to you how much of a fuss you want to make about it, but in general it's better to simply ignore it. If they are trying that hard to provoke a reaction, not giving them that satisfaction allows you to keep the moral high ground.

This is particularly important if someone chooses to storm off during the ceremony. This is most unlikely, but it may happen. In this case, your celebrant should not make a drama out of a crisis and should hopefully be experienced enough to smooth over the incident. It is best if you follow suit and don't let it spoil your big day. The difficult person's feelings are their problem; don't make them yours.

In general, however, the reaction among nonpagan relatives is usually dominated by a single emotion: curiosity. People hear all manner of things about what pagans get up to. They're usually disappointed! I've had occasions when mischievous handfastees have informed elderly relatives that everyone has to show up naked and that goat sacrifice is mandatory. More seriously, however, celebrants and handfastees alike should remember that a handfasting is an ideal "shopwindow" for paganism. It displays some of the loveliest rituals and some of the most appealing aspects of the pagan path. It is a great opportunity to show people who are unfamiliar with paganism what it's all about, and to give them the chance to ask questions.

I find that, among audiences who are unfamiliar with paganism, older relatives are usually the most impressed by these ceremonies. They relate to the idea of the four directions and the connection with the natural world. It feels old-fashioned, and they often like this. Dutch celebrant Henk Vis says, "[A] favorite moment is when the nonpagan audience understands what is happening, feels the energy, and joins in."

What If You Are Not Pagan?

It is quite customary at a handfasting for one half of the couple to be something other than pagan. Most celebrants will be accustomed to working with couples who are of mixed religions—not just those beneath the pagan banner, such as Druids and Wiccans, but also Buddhists, Catholics, atheists and agnostics, and others. Raven Kaldera and Tannin Schwartzstein's book has many examples, and this is a great book to check out if you are intending to have a "mixed marriage."[23]

Harriet Sams is based in France and works in many different areas. She is a facilitator at Healing and Ecotherapy, a writer and board member at Climate Psychology Alliance, an Earth ambassador, and a board member at Radical Joy for Hard Times. She is also a celebrant and has some advice for fellow celebrants:

> As a celebrant, I've yet to really add much spirituality and full-on pagan or other spiritual words to the couples' ceremonies, because people always say how important it is to be inclusive and not alienate the guests by being too overtly pagan. We felt that too, to be honest, how it was special to the couple and how the ritual itself could be all-inclusive and meaningful is a big issue to those creating their ritual.

23. Raven Kaldera and Tannin Schwartzstein, *Inviting Hera's Blessing: Handfasting and Wedding Rituals* (Woodbury: Llewellyn, 2003).

Location

Do you have a specific location in mind for your handfasting? A sacred circle, a temple, or another sacred space? This might affect your choice of celebrant—will you be bringing a celebrant with you, expecting someone to travel (in which case you'll need to pay travel expenses), or finding someone locally?

Since my partner Trevor and I are based in Glastonbury, we often get inquiries from people elsewhere in Britain or other countries who like the idea of getting handfasted in "pagan central." Because of the town's popularity, there is quite a high percentage of celebrants in the locality, and it isn't usually too difficult to find someone, even perhaps at short notice. If, however, you have some remote location in mind, you might have a little difficulty finding someone to conduct your ceremony—so again, make sure that you leave plenty of time to work things out.

If you are thinking of a specific location, such as woodland, is this public land or not? If it's private, you will need permission—you don't want to be thrown off by an irate landowner halfway through the ceremony. If it's public, do you mind attracting attention from passersby? Are you running the risk of breaking the law? For example, it is illegal in England to carry a knife with a blade over three inches long (although in places that are often used by pagans carrying athames, the police are often surprisingly tolerant). Are you planning to light a fire? This isn't allowed in some public parks (and you need to check with indoor venues, too, if it is permitted to light candles and/or incense burners). Make sure, whether it's a private or public location, that you follow the old adage: *leave nothing but footprints, take nothing but photos, kill nothing but time.*

Honoring the Local Spirits

Whichever location celebrants are working in, they will often like to honor the more general *genius loci*: the spirits of place. I believe that if you are working in someone else's place of residence, it's important to thank them, even if you don't know their name. Because so many spirit and god names have been lost over the centuries, in lands that have been lived in and worked on for thousands of years by many different peoples, we may not know the original names, but we can still thank the spirits of the local hills, the sea, or the nearby river. And this is something that you can do wherever you live, because those spirits, to many of us as pagans, are still there.

I also make sure that handfastees and guests notice what is around us when performing an outside ceremony. Take a look—what do you see? Which trees and flowers can you see around you? Is there any wildlife, such as birds or animals?

All of these—the birds, animals, plants, trees, and the elements themselves—have, according to many pagan paths, spirits of their own, and these can all be woven into the words of your handfasting ceremony like multicolored ribbons, threads that will settle your audience into the place and remind them of where they are. It's not just an empty field: it's a living environment thronged with presences, and you can acknowledge these as part of the ceremony itself.

If you are working in an area to which you are not indigenous, it's a good thing to research it first and get to know it a little bit. What's the folklore associated with it, if there is any? Are there any myths and legends that you can incorporate into the handfasting ceremony? Respectfully, of course—not just claiming stories and spirits as your own, but acknowledging the importance of them to the surrounding landscape.

Tips for the Celebrant

If you are the celebrant and about to undertake a handfasting, there are some basic preliminary questions to ask:

- How many prehandfasting sessions will you be having with the couple?
- Will you be writing a unique ritual for the ceremony?
- Will you be required to attend a dress rehearsal?
- Will you need to submit paperwork to a government department in countries where handfasting is a legally acknowledged ceremony?

- If you are traveling a long way, will you need to be put up in a hotel, and are you considering those costs in your budget and fee? (For example, as celebrants who ran a witchcraft shop, I had to factor in the cost of an employee's wages on the days when my partner and I were unable to run the shop because we were involved in a handfasting. When I explained this to couples, they understood completely, and I have never had an issue over the fees we charge.)

When it comes to numbers, we have done handfastings for as many as three hundred people and as few as two. The smaller handfastings are often held when there is a particular reason behind having a very private ceremony. You may, for instance, be asked to do a handfasting for a couple who are very private about their spirituality and who are not in a position to "come out of the broom closet" to friends and family. You might be asked to conduct a ceremony for someone who is already legally married to a person other than their handfasting partner and who can't obtain a divorce (I'll look at the ethics of this later on). The size of the ceremony will only be important to you as a celebrant with regard to the location and the logistics; organizing a crowd of two hundred takes a little more time than directing a single couple. My partner conducted one handfasting where the bride, a keen rider, was determined to arrive on horseback. She did so, and this was lovely, but it did require Trevor to think carefully about where several hundred people and a horse were actually going to *go* in a limited outdoor space.

Obviously, the number of people who are invited will dictate to some extent the choice of venue.

When it comes to the guests themselves and the questions they may have about paganism, our role as celebrants is not, obviously, to proselytize. We are not fundamentalists, and we do not have a mission to convert people to our religion. However, people are likely to be intrigued, and this is your chance to inform the general public, to answer any questions they may have, and to correct any misconceptions of what paganism is all about. But do discuss all this with your handfasting couple.

Conclusion

In order for your handfasting to be a success, you need to think things through and start planning well in advance. This may seem obvious, but as I've noted, some people still leave their handfasting until the last minute—with inevitable consequences. Both handfasting couples and celebrants need to make a list of every aspect of the ceremony and try to anticipate problems before they happen.

Helen Woodsford-Dean in Orkney advises,

To conduct a ceremony, you need to be a detail person. Think of EVERY-THING. The buck stops with you. If in doubt, ask and double-check. This equally applies when wedding planners are involved. Never assume. You also have to be deadline-focused; find a way to ask for feedback and directions while planning the ritual for people who are likely to be busy—too busy to think about their wedding sometimes. Say no if you can't do something or don't want to do it—this is best for your personal integrity. Be prepared to have to re-create something several times. Be prepared for odd requests.

Chapter Four

When to Get Handfasted:
The Wheel of the Year

The time of year in which you choose to hold your handfasting is obviously important. Many, but by no means all, pagans elect to be handfasted in the spring or summer months of the year—just as many brides choose the same period for conventional weddings. Beltane in May is an obvious choice, but different festivals have different meanings for various people, and Trevor and I chose to get handfasted on the winter solstice. I have done a lot of winter handfastings and several at Samhain—usually seen as a festival of the dead, but popular among Goths and others!

Some people will choose a time and date according to astrological factors; you may wish to consult a professional astrologer for this. Organizing events around the stars used to be a common practice: Queen Elizabeth I consulted magician John Dee with regard to her coronation, and weddings, too, used to be subject to divination. If astrology is your thing, your main consideration will obviously be the position of Venus, and witches/Wiccans will probably want to take the lunar cycle into consideration, too.

To an extent, your choice of time of year may depend on your choice of location. In Britain and parts of the States, the winter can be cold and wet, and this may affect your choice of whether to hold your handfasting inside or outdoors. It must be said that in the UK, the weather is a bit of a lottery, and I have conducted some very cold, damp handfastings in August and, conversely, some beautifully clear and sunlit ones around the winter solstice. It's up to you whether you want to take the risk of an outdoor handfasting—particularly one which might not have a shelter. Remember that the time of your handfasting (spring/summer or autumn/winter) and the nature of the weather of those seasons in your region will also affect your catering arrangements. If it's blisteringly hot, you'll need shade at your reception; if it's chilly and wet, you'll need undercover areas for seating and eating. It's obviously crucial to discuss this in some detail with your chosen venue, and this is one argument for using professional wedding venues to host your reception—they will have organized a lot of ceremonies and hopefully will be aware of any problems.

Take a look at what the weather is doing. Get to know your clouds and what they portend. You should be able to time your ceremony before the big wet westerly sweeps in and drenches everyone (some pagans don't mind, of course!).

You may, however, also want to consider the logistics of tying the handfasting into a seasonal celebration. German celebrant Cat Pentaberry, whom we met in our last chapter, talks about her own handfasting experience:

We wanted to have full control of all aspects. Why? Because we originally planned to have the ceremony as part of a local coven's yearly Merry Meet. We had the okay of every single member, after which it all went down in flames when the usual infighting started—in fact, the coven fell apart soon afterward. It was not a pleasant experience, and we were lucky to not have started booking the catering and so on as the cancellation was rather short notice.

Cat and her partner ended up being handfasted on the first full moon after Litha (summer solstice). Below, I will run through the pagan Wheel of the Year, considered in the light of your handfasting ceremony. What are the major festivals and the meaning and symbolism attached to each one?

Beltane: May 1

This is the pagan festival of the beginning of summer that celebrates love—the old May Day. A great many handfastings take place around this time.

The earliest mention of Beltane was in the *Sanas Chormaic*, a medieval glossary published around 900 AD that mentions "lucky fires." It seems to have been a fire festival involving two big bonfires through which cattle were herded to protect them before they were taken up to their summer pastures. These bonfires may have been linked to a god named Bel, Bil, or Baal.

In ancient Celtic times, this festival may not have had the same meaning that it has today. The Celts may have held that this was a time of year when the veil between the worlds was thin, a time when spirits, ghosts, and fairy folk were abroad—a chancy time when it may have been safer to stay at home! In traditional folklore throughout the medieval and Elizabethan periods, May Eve had many of the connotations we now associate with Hallowe'en. The Welsh festival Calan Mai is linked to this kind of supernatural activity, and according to the tale of Culhwch and Olwen, the heroes Gwythyr and Gwyn ap Nudd are fated to do battle on May Eve—summer defeating winter. But in the early nineteenth century, festivals involving cattle and fires were held throughout Ireland. Women jumped the fire to ensure that they would meet a husband, and wives did so to ensure fertility.

Primroses were scattered over the doorstep in Ireland and, less pleasantly, any hares found among the cattle were killed, in case they were witches in disguise. In Scotland, rowan crosses were put over the door to protect the inhabitants, and rowan branches were used widely at this time to protect against negative magic.

Many of these associations have now fallen away, although in Glastonbury people often comment on a disturbed, disruptive energy around Beltane. (A friend of ours arrived in Glastonbury for the first time on May Eve in the 1970s and, in the twilight of the Tor, heard men and horses and the clash of armor, but there was nothing to be seen—perhaps the Wild Hunt riding out?)

Driving cattle through the smoke was supposed to be purifying. One of the legends of Saint Patrick says that he lit the Beltane fire on Tara before the king had a chance to do so—this was a clear message to the Irish people that Patrick intended to usurp the royal power.

Another custom among the Irish was the creation of a "May bush"—a decorated hawthorn bush that was placed outside the dwelling. In my family (Welsh), it was always considered unlucky to bring flowering hawthorn into the house: perhaps as a tree of the goddess, she needs it outside! It is also not a certainty that hawthorn will be out in time for Beltane—although when I wrote this in April, May was already flowering.

Later customs included bathing one's face in the dew on May morning (more for women than for men!) to purify the complexion. A nice custom to follow, perhaps, on the morning of your handfasting. And you may choose to decorate your handfasting site with a Beltane bush, too!

Summer Solstice: June 21

The word *solstice* comes from the Latin words for "sun" and "to stand still," so some people refer to it as the "sunstanding." We may also know it simply as Midsummer (which technically is Saint John's Eve on June 24) or the Longest Day. Again, it's a popular time of year for handfastings.

The summer solstice is one of the four main quarter days of the pagan year—the time when the day is longest. As part of the ritual Wheel of the Year, it is held by author Robert Graves, among others, to be the point at which the Holly King symbolically triumphs over the Oak King (if Holly is the darker power, and Oak is light, then this makes sense, as the Oak's days are now numbered—from now on, the days start to get shorter).

Like most pagan festivals, this has a Christian equivalent in Saint John's Eve at Midsummer (June 24). The uncanny light in which Midsummer was viewed is clear from one of Shakespeare's most famous plays—*A Midsummer Night's Dream*—in which magic and mayhem rule and the fairy folk wreak havoc on mortals. To protect against negative magic at this time, people wore protective herbs, including the plant known as "chase-devil," or Saint John's Wort, which in its modern equivalent is indeed used to chase away depression.

If you have a bush of Saint John's Wort, then you can go out on Midsummer Eve and gather some of the little yellow flowers, then place them in a small phial or bottle with some oil (ordinary sunflower oil is fine and quite appropriate). Steep it in sunlight for a week or two and use it in solar magic. You can wear it for luck in your summer handfasting (do a skin test first, as Saint John's Wort can sensitize you to sunlight, and you may want to put it on a scrap of handkerchief instead). As one of the main points of the pagan summer calendar and a time of maximum light, the summer solstice is a magical time to be handfast.

Lammas: August 1

Lughnasadh (pronounced *loon-a-sath* or *loonasa*) is the great harvest festival of the pagan calendar: a time of fertility, fruitfulness, and celebration. It's commensurate with the English harvest festival of Lammas. Paganism was seen as a fertility religion by writers such as Frazer and Graves, but we don't have any real evidence for this (although it does seem fairly natural for agricultural societies to be concerned with fruitfulness and abundance). *Lughnasadh* refers to the bright god Lugh, whereas *Lammas* is said to come from the Anglo-Saxon *hlaef mass*, or "loaf mass," when the bread from the first wheat of the year was eaten.

This festival does, however, have a darker side: that of sacrifice and death. The old folk song "John Barleycorn" sums this up—the corn is sown, sprouts, ripens, and is eventually harvested, and it is this process of harvesting that represents the dark side of sacrifice. It was, in Irish mythology, said to have been started by the god Lugh as a funeral feast for his dead mother, Tailtiu, who expired of exhaustion after preparing the Irish plains for agriculture (anyone who has a garden and who has reached this stage of the summer will sympathize!). At these feasts, games and horse races were held.

The Romans held it as a festival in Lyon, whose name derives from the Gaulish Lugdunum (Lugh's Fortress), and August 1 is still the national holiday of Switzerland, celebrated by lighting bonfires.

It is not clear how widely festivities at this time of year were spread throughout the Celtic world. There is reference to it in ancient Irish texts, but it does not seem to have been a particularly English celebration. As Lammas, however, it is still commemorated within the Christian church.

These days, Lammas is celebrated with bonfires and by decorating the house with corn dollies or sheaves of wheat. At this depth of the summer, Lammas is a popular choice for handfastings. It's a high point of the summer, and the weather is usually good wherever you are—thus, a positive time to hold your handfasting ceremony outdoors.

Autumn Equinox: September 21

The autumn equinox, sometimes named "Mabon," is a time when the year is once again in balance, with day and night of equal length. However, it is a time when the tides of the year are on the change, ebbing rather than rising, and taking anything unwanted with them. Thus, it is a good time to release anything for which you have no further need, as well as to celebrate the harvest that the year has brought—you can also regard Mabon as the Harvest Home and treat your wedding as part of the yearly harvest. You may wish to bake a loaf of bread for your handfasting, perhaps in the shape of a corn plait, or decorate the house with bunches of autumn leaves; either would be very appropriate for a handfasting at this time of year.

The name "Mabon" comes from the young god in Welsh legends, the son of the Modron (the names just mean "son" and "mother"). The Mabon goes missing, and his mother frantically searches for him, enlisting the help of various people (such as King Arthur's knights, depending on which legend you follow) and the eldest animals and birds of Britain. This story resembles the myth of Persephone, who is snatched into the underworld and whose mother, Demeter, searches for her while the Earth turns to winter. But we should note that "Mabon" is a recent name for this festival, deriving from the writing of Aidan Kelly, and that the original legend is set in January.

Samhain: October 31

Samhain, the pagan equivalent of Hallowe'en, is the great festival of the dead and of honoring the ancestors. The history of Samhain is murky, like the origins of all festivals. Conventional wisdom has it that Christianity "stole" many of the old pagan holidays. With Samhain, it's particularly difficult to know what this time of year represented. Contrary to popular myth, there's little evidence that the ancient Celts regarded it as the start of the New Year, as modern pagans do now. It seems to have been a festival based on the slaughter of cattle for the winter season. Sometimes tribes lit hilltop fires, sometimes not; it varied across Britain and Ireland. It seems likely that modern pagans have taken many traditions and customs from the Christian festival of All Soul's, rather than the other way around.

Regardless of where the festival comes from, many pagans today treat it as the start of the New Year and use this dark time to honor their ancestors and anyone who died during the previous year. In my personal working group, we hold a ritual in which a symbolic gateway is opened between the world of the living and the world of the dead, and the spirits of those who have died are invited to come through into the circle, purely so that they might be honored. A member of the group dresses in a black veil as the Cailleach, the crone, and she moves around the circle, asking each person what this festival means to them. It is a powerful way of facing one's own death.

Despite this, many handfastings take place around Samhain, as many pagans regard it as a numinous and important time of the year, and I quite often act as a celebrant for couples at this particular time. If you treat it as the New Year, then a handfasting is a great start to the year, too.

Winter Solstice: December 21

This solstice season is equivalent to the pagan celebration of Christmas and shares many characteristics with that festival. It is a celebration of fire and light, where evergreens are brought into the house and feasts are prepared. The origins of this festival are lost, but they are probably ancient and may relate to the stories told about the origins of the birth of the god Mithras, who was born in December in a cave. The emperor Aurelian established December 25 as the birth of the Invincible Sun.

To modern pagans, this is the time when the goddess gives birth to a shining son, the Mabon.

This season was celebrated in Rome as the Saturnalia, a period when the normal social order was reversed and masters waited on servants. We do not do this today, but some aspects of this old Roman festival would be familiar to us—for instance, bringing evergreens, such as bay and laurel, into our homes.

The winter solstice is also the opposite of the summer solstice: now, the Holly King and the Oak King fight once more, and this time the Oak King wins, reigning over the world until summer. From now on, evenings will start to lighten a little. Pagans gather at Stonehenge or Newgrange and other ancient sites, many of which were aligned to receive the first light of the Midwinter sun.

Some pagans like to use this season as a setting for their handfasting ceremony. You may wish to work with the Holly King and the Oak King, visualizing their ritual battle. Or you may choose to honor the goddess at this time of year in her role as the one who gives birth to the sacred child, the Mabon. Many pagans believe that this is where the original legend of Christ's birth came from—in a cave, at Midwinter, the Child of Light is born. Light a white candle for her, symbolizing the return of the sun from the winter darkness, and make an offering of honey or mead. You may wish to work with the sun itself, rising at dawn on the morning of the winter solstice at a sacred site or somewhere near you to watch the sun rise above the horizon as you carry out your handfasting.

Imbolc: February 1st

Imbolc (the name possibly means "ewe's milk") is the festival dedicated to the Goddess Bride. Its name comes from one of the poems of the Ulster Cycle, *The Wooing of Emer*, in which the heroine Emer mentions that at Imbolc the ewes are milked at spring's beginning. However, etymologists are not certain that this is the origin of the word, and it may derive from a much older term.

An Irish deity, Bride (who may also be Saint Bridget) is the flame-haired goddess of the forge, healing, and poetry. She is accompanied by swans, lambs, and snowdrops. Under her name Brigid, which means "fiery arrow," she is a deity associated with fire, so we also burn candles to welcome her, and in the Christian calendar, this date is known as "Candlemas." She also has a more martial aspect and is sometimes connected with war, so you have a number of aspects to choose from when connecting with this deity!

Bride is associated with Kildare—there is a shrine to the saint here—and with Glastonbury, where she is supposed to have resided at a shrine on Bride's Mound.

In Ireland, the saint was supposed to visit virtuous households on her night, so families would welcome her in after a special supper. Sometimes a four-armed "Bride's Cross" would be made out of rushes.

If you wish to do a ritual before your February handfasting to celebrate Imbolc, buy a small bowl of snowdrops and place them on your altar, if you have one, or in a special place. Light white candles. If you carve or make dolls, you can also make a representation of the Goddess Bride and place her in a small basket—this is an old Scottish custom known as "Bride's Bed." In the Outer Hebrides, a representation of Bride would be made and decked with shells, primroses, snowdrops, and crystals, with a bright crystal above her heart. Take a few minutes to ask the goddess for her guidance for your handfasting ceremony.

Spring Equinox: March 21

The spring equinox, which falls around March 21, is one of the two days of equal length (the other being, obviously, the autumn equinox on September 21). Pagans are not the only people who celebrate around this time—the Islamic festival of Navruz falls around this date, and so does a very ancient Egyptian festival called Sham El Nessim. The Jewish Passover is also celebrated on the first full moon following the first new moon after the equinox.

Witches and Wiccans usually use the name Ostara for this festival, although Druids may know it as Alban Eilir. It is not a major festival (unlike, say, Samhain or the summer solstice), but it does mark the Wheel of the Year, and many of us like an excuse to celebrate the arrival of spring! As with Beltane, some people want to become handfasted now, when the year is turning toward the summer months and life is starting to renew itself.

To many pagans, the spring festival of Ostara is now symbolized by the hare and by the egg. It's almost as though the pagan community is drawing upon some of the traditions of Easter—which is, of course, a specifically Christian festival, one of the only ones that does not have a historical crossover of some kind with pagan practices. But is this really the case?

It's unclear where the name comes from. Modern pagan convention holds that it is derived from the goddess Ostara, or Eostre, whose name is supposed to be related to "oestrogen" (in fact, this is not true). But she's only mentioned once in a text by the Venerable Bede and might either be a deity of the dawn or of a German river valley! Her popularity came about through the brothers Grimm, who cite her as a goddess, and she then runs through modern pagan writing as a distinct deity!

Whatever her origins, the festival that we celebrate is now associated with the hare and the moon—people often ask me why there are so many representations of the hare in Glastonbury, and it's partly due to the old tradition that witches had the power to turn themselves into hares. (The old stories of a man who sees a hare raiding his garden and shoots it in the leg. Next day, granny's got a limp!) This may be because wounded hares scream like an injured human being, so perhaps the association was made as a result of this.

The spring equinox is a lovely time to become handfasted, with the signs of spring all around you: a season of renewal and hope. As the poet Wordsworth wrote:

> All things that love the sun are out of doors;
> The sky rejoices in the morning's birth;
> The grass is bright with rain-drops; -on the moors
> The hare is running races in her mirth;
> And with her feet she from the plashy earth
> Raises a mist; that, glittering in the sun,
> Runs with her all the way, wherever she doth run.[24]

24. William Wordsworth, "Resolution and Independence," *Poetry Foundation*, accessed November 3, 2020, https://www.poetryfoundation.org/poems/45545/resolution -and-independence.

Conclusion

There are advantages to holding your handfasting at any of the main pagan festivals: from the coziness of the winter celebrations to the joyful summer sun at Midsummer and Lughnasadh, from the beauty and fruitfulness of autumn to the return of new life in the spring (or the other way around if you're in the Southern Hemisphere, of course). Honoring the symbols and correspondences of the time of year gives additional meaning and depth to your handfasting ceremony, marking it as a seasonal ritual that is truly connected to the pagan Wheel of the Year.

There may be a time of year that is particularly meaningful to you, or your choice of season may be dictated by logistics. Whatever time of the year you choose, there is plenty of scope for making your handfasting a truly seasonal celebration. It's a great opportunity to weave the customs and symbols of the season into your own special day.

Chapter Five

The Ceremony

The big question that most handfastees ask their celebrant, especially if they are new to paganism, is about the ceremony itself. What form does it take? What will you have to do? Is it very complicated? Your celebrant should go through each stage of the handfasting ceremony with you, and I also usually send handfasting couples a sample ritual so that they can see whether it resonates with them, but we will go through all the steps below.

What handfastees want will depend to a large extent on how experienced they are already in participating in ritual. Some of our clients have been pagans for many years and are accustomed to taking part in many different types of ritual. If you fall into this category, you will probably want to have a hand in crafting your handfasting ritual yourself, and some firm ideas of what you'd prefer.

If you are new to handfasting and paganism, however (perhaps you just like the idea of a handfasting but haven't committed to any particular pagan path), you may want to rely more heavily on your celebrant to organize your ritual for you. In this case, your celebrant will go through each aspect of the ceremony carefully with you.

This chapter gives you some ideas as to what to expect in your handfasting ceremony. In it, I outline a sample ceremony: this is a standard type of magical ritual tailored for a handfasting and can be tweaked depending on which pagan path you follow. One further note: in chapter 10, we look at setting up a ritual and the things you will need, such as candles, incense, and oils. You might like to look at both chapters when you and your celebrant are putting your handfasting ceremony together.

Opening Your Ceremony

The celebrant will take their knife, athame, or wand (we'll look at ritual tools in a later chapter). They will face east and hold up the athame (or staff or sword) in their working hand (i.e., if they're left-handed, they will use that hand). Holding their other hand down toward the ground, they will ask you to picture a thread of energy coming up from the earth, through their hand, across their body, and down the arm that holds the athame, to be projected outward through the tip of the knife. It doesn't matter what color you imagine the energy to be—white, or blue, or gold, for instance. The celebrant will then walk clockwise (sunwise) around the perimeter, drawing the circle in the air, usually just above head height.

Some people express intentions as they do this—for example, if a celebrant is doing a ritual dedicated to handfasting, they might explicitly say what the ritual is about ("On this night, at this new moon, I call upon the lunar powers to watch over this handfasting between [*names of couple*]")—until they have reached the east again and the circle is complete. Usually, the person drawing the circle imagines that thread of energy emerging from the tip of the wand or finger and forming a circle, perhaps as a thread of white light, or neon blue, or gold.

Can You Step Out of the Circle?

Yes. Sometimes something just happens outside the circle (crying child, howling dog) and you have to deal with it. Most celebrants will "draw" a doorway in the air and step through it to show that they're aware that it's sacred space. Don't just bolt through it after your fleeing child, though! Some Wiccan elders suggest taking the circle down and redrawing it. But don't obsess about breaking the circle; you won't be struck by lightning if it happens.

How Big Does the Circle Have to Be?

Big enough in which to work comfortably, but it depends on the size of your room or the outdoor space. You can project energy as far as you need to—not miles to the far-off horizon, but as far as is needed to accommodate a big group of people if necessary. More traditional Wiccans hold that the circle must be nine feet in diameter (nine is the number traditionally associated with the moon). If you want to do this, cut a cord four and a half feet in length, place it in the middle of your potential circle, and measure outward. Your celebrant might also delineate the working circle in white chalk or with a white rope.

Can a Circle Be Drawn Outside, Without an Altar?

By all means. There's nothing to say you have to work inside or outside.

Why Do We Draw It Sunwise?

It's that connection with the natural world, the way the sun travels. There's an old view in traditional witchcraft that to walk anticlockwise, or "widdershins," is unlucky, and this view has somehow become ingrained in our inner selves—at least when drawing the circle. Unwinding it is another matter, as we will see.

What is important is the **connection** your celebrant and you yourself make between earth and air and the wider world. You're delineating it with energy that comes from the earth, not from yourself, to make sacred space. Magic is all about making connections, and this basic part of ritual is an aspect of that.

Consecrating with Water

Once the circle has been drawn (using energies of earth and air), it's customary to **consecrate** it with water and fire. I usually do water first, out of a feeling that if you consecrate with fire first, the water puts it out!

The celebrant will take a chalice or cup full of water and go around the circle, from east, then to south, then to west, then to north, and back to the east, sunwise. They will typically flick a few drops as they go—with a group, it's customary to anoint each person's brow as they go around. They may speak as they do so: *I consecrate this circle with the element of water, the purifier, the cleanser, element of river and spring and sea, of the falling rain*—or whatever words come most naturally to mind.

As the celebrant does this, don't just concentrate on their words, but imagine water in the form of rain, or mist, or even salt spray.

Consecrating with Fire

Now do the same thing with incense, either with a joss stick or incense in a censer. Again, your celebrant will usually say something along the lines of, "I consecrate this circle with the element of fire, the energizer, element of noonday and high summer and the leaping flame in the hearth..." Do the same for fire as you did for water as you are listening to the celebrant; imagine the light of the sun, or the heat of flame.

Calling the Quarters

It's usual for most pagan rituals to "call the quarters" at this point, locating the circle and placing you firmly within your ritual space, and handfasting is no exception. I will begin with the general properties of the quarters and then move on to the specifics.

There are many correspondences and many deities, so I have included only a few here. Please also bear in mind, especially if you are new to this and have been asked to officiate as a quarter officer at a handfasting, that correspondences might vary, and some of them are not very old, so they are not set in stone.

East

Time: Dawn

Season: Spring

Element: Air (fire in some systems, in which case just swap air and fire correspondences around)

Ritual Tool: Athame (or wand, if using fire in this quarter)

Zodiac Signs: Gemini, Libra, Aquarius

Color: White/pale yellow

Animals: The hawk, birds in general

Goddesses/Gods: Bride, Mercury, Thoth

South

Time: Noon

Season: Summer

Element: Fire (air in some systems)

Ritual Tool: Wand (or athame, if using air in this quarter)

Zodiac Signs: Aries, Leo, Sagittarius

Color: Gold/red

Animals: The stag, the fox, the lion, the dragon

Goddesses/Gods: Lugh, Bel, Hephaestus, Hestia

West

Time: Evening

Season: Autumn

Element: Water

Ritual Tool: Chalice

Zodiac Signs: Cancer, Scorpio, Pisces

Color: Green/blue/sea colors

Animals: The cow, the salmon of wisdom from Celtic legend, seals, and
water creatures

Goddesses/Gods: Rhiannon, Isis, Danu, Llyr/Mannanan, Osiris

North

Time: Midnight

Season: Winter

Element: Earth

Ritual Tool: Pentacle, dish of salt, crystals

Zodiac Signs: Taurus, Virgo, Capricorn

Color: Black/indigo blue/dark green

Animals: Bear, badger, snake

Goddesses/Gods: Arianrhod, Frey, Freya, Odin, Morrigan

Tip for the Celebrant: Evoking Spirits of Place

To me, this is one of the most important aspects of calling the quarters and is very rarely done. This may mean that we depart from more standard systems of correspondences—for example, Gwyn (as a deity of the underworld) would traditionally be associated with the north, but since he is supposed to live beneath the Tor, and that is east of us, we call him in the east.

I live just west of Glastonbury, and so when I call the quarters, this is how it goes:

East: I call upon the spirits of East—spirits of spring, of dawn, of morning! I call upon the spirits of the air, spirits of the winds! I call upon the hawk, the peregrine soaring in the clear skies. I call upon the spirits of the Tor, that rises to the east of these Levels, of Gwyn the Hunter, of the Goddess Bride, of Orion, who strides from the sides of the Tor! Behold! The gateway to the East is open!

South: I call upon the spirits of the South—spirits of summer, of noonday, of the sun at its zenith! I call upon the spirits of fire, spirits of flame and simmering heat! I call upon the great stag running, on the fox in the woods. I call upon the spirits of the Polden Hills, the low hills, the Quantocks. Behold! The gateway to the South is open!

West: I call upon the spirits of the West—spirits of river and spring, spirits of evening and autumn. I call upon the spirits of the crashing seas, of twilight, of the salmon leaping in the pool of wisdom, of the spotted cow beside the darkening pool. I call upon the spirits of Severn Sea and Severn Shore, of Brean and Brent Knoll! Behold! The gateway to the West is open!

North: I call upon the spirits of the North—spirits of winter, spirits of midnight, spirits of the iron cold. I call upon the spirits of earth, of standing stone. I call upon the Great Bear in the starry heavens, of badger beneath the earth. I call upon the spirits of the Mendips, spirits of cave and gorge, spirits of copper and tin, spirits of the high bare hills! Behold! The gateway to the North is open!

This anchors your ritual space, your sacred space, in its environment and honors the spirits around it. Note that I have used a certain kind of phrasing. I've said that there's no single right way to do ritual, but when you look at older forms of magic, they speak of "summoning" the spirits of the quarters. I've always felt that this is a bit rude. I always imagine those spirits sitting with their feet up and a cup of tea, when suddenly some mortal appears in the front room bellowing "I summon thee!" If you believe in deities as beings external to yourself, you are not dealing with beings who are under your control. They can, and do, bite back, just like any other wild thing when it's treated with disrespect.

You do not have to use the "behold!" invocation, either. It is used in Druidic ritual, but you could just state that, for example, the northern gate or door or portal is open.

As with the consecrations, the power of calling the quarters does not lie in the words you use (though in public ritual, it does help if they are opened and closed fairly dramatically—but public ritual, especially handfastings, contain a strong quality of public theater, and not everyone takes to the "am dram" character of some ritual work!). Its power lies in the images you invoke—when I call the east, for instance, I see in my mind's eye a high mountain scene, glimpsed between two birch trees. A hunting peregrine soars up into the clear morning air, and the atmosphere is cold in the early light. Snowdrops ring the foot of the birches, and the morning star is still a lamp in the sky.

But that's my own vision. Other people may have a very different visualization—of a gate of clear quartz, for example. What you are doing, however you envision it, is building up your own relationship with the quarter and the elements associated with it.

The Central Ceremony

What happens in this section of the ritual will vary depending on the spiritual tradition of the couple. You will need to discuss this with your celebrant. For example:

- Are you going to be ritually "challenged" by the celebrant? Is there a set ritual involved? (For example, "Do you come here of your own free will?")
- Which gods/goddesses/spirits should your celebrant call upon?
- How is the cord to be tied?
- Are there any particular symbols to be included in the ceremony?
- How do you want the celebrant to close your circle? Do you, for instance, want to send the energy out to enchant the world?
- If this is in a country where handfasting is legally binding, which words and phrases will your celebrant need to incorporate?

In addition to these elements, which you may or may not wish to include, there are usually some other set actions in this central part of the ceremony:

- Vows (the main focus of the ritual)
- Binding hands
- Exchanging rings (some handfastings incorporate this, while some do not)

How to "Tie the Knot"

It's a good idea to rehearse this, as it's not a natural thing to do and most people haven't done it before. It's relatively easy to exchange rings, but handfastings often involve a moment of slight chaos when people get their hands round the "wrong" way, or don't know quite what they're supposed to do. To prevent the celebrant having to seize your hands and place them together, in general it is

Bride/groom: left hand

Bride/groom: right hand

Or you can cross hands so that you are reaching across each other and forming a figure eight (also known as the infinity symbol, which appears above the head of the Magician in some tarot decks).

Once your hands are clasped, the celebrant can either wind the cord or ribbon around your hands or, as in the royal wedding, simply drape it across your joined hands.

Usually, you do not remain bound for long. I tend to ask the couple to stay tied together for as long as it takes to jump over the broomstick (if they choose to do that). This symbolizes the gateway into their new lives, and once they have done this, I untie the cord, saying,

I unbind your hands, but may you remain bound in the nonmaterial world.

And this conveys to everyone that they are, indeed, handfasted.

Most couples like to take the handfasting cord away with them and perhaps tie it to the broomstick, place it on a household altar, or hang it on the wall.

In some traditions, there is more than one binding. For instance, you may wish to ask a series of ritual questions, such as, "Do you promise to honor [x]?" Once both people have answered, the first binding is made, then a second binding after a second question, and so forth. At the end, the cord itself is made up of a series of smaller cords.

The couple may want to have other elements in the central ceremony. For example,

- Readings or poems (read either by the couple or by guests)
- Songs and music
- Visualizations
- Tarot or rune reading
- Meditation

This account, for instance, was from one of our contributors, who chose to remain anonymous:

My favorite part of the ceremony was a meditation we all did. My partner and I stood in the middle of the circle holding hands. The others stood around us. Rather than pledging to be together for a certain amount of time, we asked that we love each other forever, no matter what. This is what we all meditated on and sent energy to. Our rings were inscribed with "love forever." It was one of the most special moments of my life.

Closing the Ceremony

Once you have done all that you wish to do within your ritual, you need to close it down. This is straightforward. Starting in the north (although some celebrants begin in the east), your celebrant will begin the winding down by thanking the spirits of each of the quarters. For example,

North: I thank the spirits of the North—spirits of winter, spirits of midnight, spirits of the iron cold. I thank the spirits of earth, of standing stone. I thank the Great Bear in the starry heavens, of badger beneath the earth. I thank the spirits of the Mendips, spirits of cave and gorge, spirits of copper and tin, spirits of the high bare hills! Behold! The gateway to the North is now closed!

… and so on for **West, South,** and **East.** Once the quarters have been closed, the circle itself is now closed, beginning in the east but moving anticlockwise to "unwind" your circle. The celebrant will then reverse the casting that they made at the start of the ritual, picturing energy passing through their athame, back down their arm and across their body, and into the earth.

At this point, if the couple are actually going to jump the broomstick, I invite them to do that at this point, so that as they jump, they are not breaking the circle.

That's it! You may wish to tweak this basic ritual to fit your own tradition, and I will give some examples below.

Example 1: Wiccan Handfasting

High Priest/Priestess (HP): Let he who wishes to be handfasted approach me now.

[Groom steps forward.]

HP: Let she who wishes to be handfasted approach me now.

[Bride steps forward.]

HP speaks to the coven/group: Does anyone here have any objections to this couple being handfasted? If so, speak now, or forever hold it to your heart.

[Short pause.]

HP addresses the spirits: Should any of the Spirits here gathered have objections to this union, now is the time to make it known.

[Short pause.]

HP speaks to groom: Do you, [groom], stand in our presence of your own free will to seek union with [bride]?

Groom: I come here of my own free will and desire.

HP to groom: Do you pledge that this union will be one of perfect love and perfect trust?

Groom: I so pledge.

HP to bride: Do you, [bride], stand in our presence of your own free will to seek union with [groom]?

Bride: I come here of my own free will and desire.

HP to bride: Do you pledge that this union will be one of perfect love and perfect trust?

Bride: I so pledge.

[It is time for the Blessings of the Elementals, the Goddess, and the God. Bride and groom walk over to the altar.]

HP picks up the bowl of salt and holds it up: Be with us here, spirits of Earth. Let your strength and consistency belong to this couple for so long as they desire to remain together.

HP raises up the censer: Be with us here, spirits of Air, grant that the paths of communication be open for so long as these two desire to remain together.

HP raises the bowl of water: Be with us here, oh spirits of Water, grant [groom] and [bride] the deepest of love and richness of body, soul, and spirit for so long as they desire to remain together.

HP picks up the red candle sitting on the altar and holds it up: Be with us here, oh spirits of Fire, grant that the fire of passion belong to this couple for so long as these two desire to remain together.

HP takes up the two silver candlesticks and holds them up: Blessed Goddess and mighty God, grant to [bride] and [groom] before us your eternal love and protection. Blessed Be.

HP turns to bride: Do you truly desire to handfast [groom]?

Bride: I do.

HP: Then pledge now your troth to him!

Bride: I pledge my troth to you, [groom].

HP now turns to groom: Do you truly desire to handfast [bride]?

Groom: I pledge my troth.

HP: Then pledge now your troth to her.

Groom: [Bride], I pledge my troth. My heart and my love are yours.

HP holds up the wand with the rings: Place your right hand over this wand and ring, his hand over hers.

   [Bride and groom do so.]

HP: As you have stated your desire to be united, one with the other, take now these rings and place them upon each other's finger, as pledge and testimony to your love and commitment to each other.

   [Bride and groom do so.]

HP: Above you are the stars
   Below you are the stones
   As time does pass, remember

Like a star should your love be constant
Like a stone should your love be firm
Be close, but not too close
Possess one another, yet be understanding
Have patience with each other
Be free and giving of affection and warmth
Make love often and sensuously to one another
Have no fear and let not the ways or words
of the unenlightened give you unease.
For the Goddess and the God are with you always.[25]

[HP crosses the couple's wrists and ties them loosely with the handfasting cord.]

HP: As your wrists are tied by this cord, may it be a prelude to the flowering of your lives together, and a fond remembrance of this handfasting. Also may it symbolize the bonding of your souls, your energy, and your life force; that throughout your life together, you may know of nothing but each other's joy and love, in perfect balance and peace.

[It's time to jump the broomstick, and the couple do so.]

HP: By jumping the broom together, you have proven that you can work as a single mind and spirit. Therefore, let the physical bonds of the hand-fasting be removed and saved as a reminder of this joyous day. But ever remember, the spiritual bonds will always remain. By the power vested in me as Priest/Priestess of the Wicca, we do declare to all assembled here, in the presence of the Ancient Ones, that you are husband and wife.

Example 2: Heathen Handfasting

HP: Let [bride and groom] approach the circle!

[The couple do so. HP bars their way with a sword.]

---

25. Ed Fitch, "Traditional Pagan Blessing, Spiritual Love Poems and Readings," accessed November 3, 2020, https://www.churchofancientways.org.

HP: Do you, [groom], come here of your own free will?

Groom: I do!

HP: And do you, [bride], come here of your own free will, also?

Bride: I do!

HP: Then we shall begin.

[HP raises the sword, circling around the assembled guests. HP calls upon Freya and on Iduna. HP takes the handfasting cord and, holding it, asks the couple to relate their vows.]

Bride: [Groom], in the name of Iduna, lady of apples, lady of the hearth, I wish to share my hearth with thee. Thou art the center of my life and the center of my home.

Groom: In the name of Thor, lady [bride], may my strength be ever at your hand. Thou are my beloved and shall ever be.

[HP binds their hands with a handfasting cord.]

HP: I call upon Sif of the Golden Hair, wife of mighty Thor, Swan Maid and Mistress of the Hearth. May you bestow your blessings upon this handfasting, and upon our friends and fellow warriors [bride and groom]!

[The couple each select a rune.]

HP: May this couple, [bride and groom], be handfast in the sight of the gods and goddesses!

Example 3: Druidic Handfasting

HP to assembly: Take one deep breath for the earth beneath your feet. Feel the energy that lies within this ancient land passing up through the soles of your feet, all the way up your body, and breathe out. Then take one deep breath for the sky above you. Feel the energy that lies in the sunlight and the morning air passing down through the crown of your head, all the way up your body, and breathe out. Then take one deep breath for the seas that surround these islands. Feel the energy that occupies the water, the symbol of love, that surrounds us, all the way through your body, and breathe out.

We are now going to perform what's known in Druidry as the Call to Peace.

[HP faces north, south, west, and east in turn.]

HP: May there be Peace in the North.

May there be Peace in the South.

May there be Peace in the West.

May there be Peace in the East.

May there be Peace throughout the whole world.

[The assembly repeats this. HP draws a circle and consecrates it.]

HP: I consecrate this circle with the element of water, the purifier, the cleanser, element of river and spring and sea, of the falling rain ...

[HP takes up some incense.]

HP: I consecrate this circle with the element of fire, the energizer, the brightener, element of the sun ...

[HP finishes the consecration.]

HP: We're now going to perform the Calling of the Quarters.

Quarter officer of the East: I call upon the spirits of East—spirits of spring, of dawn, of morning! I call upon the spirits of the air, spirits of the winds! I call upon the hawk, the peregrine soaring in the clear skies. Behold! The gateway to the East is open!

Assembly: The gateway to the East is open!

Quarter officer of the South: I call upon the spirits of the South—spirits of summer, of noonday, of the sun at its zenith! I call upon the spirits of fire, spirits of flame and simmering heat! I call upon the great stag running, on the fox in the woods. Behold! The gateway to the South is open!

Assembly: The gateway to the South is open!

Quarter officer of the West: I call upon the spirits of the West—spirits of river and spring, spirits of evening and autumn. I call upon the spirits of the crashing seas, of twilight, of the salmon leaping in the pool of wisdom, of the spotted cow beside the darkening pool. Behold! The gateway to the West is open!

Assembly: The gateway to the West is open!

Quarter officer of the North: I call upon the spirits of the North—spirits of winter, spirits of midnight, spirits of the iron cold. I call upon the spirits of earth, of standing stone. I call upon the Great Bear in the starry heavens, of badger beneath the earth. Behold! The gateway to the North is open!

Assembly: The gateway to the North is open!

HP: We are here today to celebrate the handfasting of [bride and groom]. We ask all here to bear witness. And now we shall begin.

   [HP invites the bride and groom to say their vows.]

Bride: In the name of the old gods and the great goddess, I vow to honor and love you, [groom], for as long as love shall last.

Groom: In the name of the old gods and the great goddess, I vow to honor and love you, [bride], for as long as love shall last.

HP: Hold out your hands.

   [They do so.]

HP: [Bride and groom], I am binding your hands to celebrate the binding of your love. May you be handfast for as long as your love shall last. Now let us close our circle.

Quarter officer of the North: I call upon the spirits of the North—spirits of winter, spirits of midnight, spirits of the iron cold. I call upon the spirits of earth, of standing stone. I call upon the Great Bear in the starry heavens, of badger beneath the earth. Thank you for watching over this handfasting! Behold! The gateway to the North is closed!

Assembly: The gateway to the North is closed!

Quarter officer of the West: I call upon the spirits of the West—spirits of river and spring, spirits of evening and autumn. I call upon the spirits of the crashing seas, of twilight, of the salmon leaping in the pool of wisdom, of the spotted cow beside the darkening pool. Thank you for watching over this handfasting! Behold! The gateway to the West is closed!

Assembly: The gateway to the West is closed!

Quarter officer of the South: I call upon the spirits of the South—spirits of summer, of noonday, of the sun at its zenith! I call upon the spirits of fire, spirits of flame and simmering heat! I call upon the great stag running, on the fox in the woods. Thank you for watching over this handfasting! Behold! The gateway to the South is closed!

Assembly: The gateway to the South is closed!

Quarter officer of the East: I call upon the spirits of East—spirits of spring, of dawn, of morning! I call upon the spirits of the air, spirits of the winds! I call upon the hawk, the peregrine soaring in the clear skies. Thank you for watching over this handfasting! Behold! The gateway to the East is closed!

Assembly: The gateway to the East is closed!

[HP closes the circle, beginning in the east and moving anticlockwise to "unwind" the circle.]

HP: Let our ritual be closed upon the mundane plane, but may it remain forever within our hearts!

Your Post-Covid Handfasting

When I started writing this book, it did not enter my head to include advice about how to hold a handfasting during a pandemic. Anyway! There went that…

In 2020, everything changed. Many weddings and handfastings had to be postponed or cancelled. (As I wrote this, I was in email correspondence with a disappointed handfasting couple who had to put off their big day in September 2020; they were hoping to hold it at the Chalice Well, but although the venue was open, the number of elderly relatives who were still shielding halved the numbers of guests, and they decided to put it off, rather than go ahead.)

If an outbreak of Covid or another pandemic throws a spanner into the works, what action should you take? If you need to cancel the proceedings, British magazine *The Tatler* suggests that you call guests personally and explain the situation to them. Similarly, you should call them personally if the ceremony has to be cut down in size and you need to "disinvite" guests. This is a nightmare but may realistically have to be done. Mail any handfasting favors to disinvited guests. Encourage guests not to bring gifts on the day if you are worried about infection, and consider installing hand sanitizer stations (the venue is likely to do this for you). Include any social distancing guidelines in the directions you send to guests.

In any case, the focus should be on the ceremony itself rather than on the guest list and the reception. Many couples have had to cut their guest lists—Princess Beatrice had a small private ceremony for her 2020 wedding, for example. In general, handfasting couples tend to have a focus on the spiritual side of the ceremony as it is, and you can always suggest to pagan guests that they hold a private household ritual on your behalf on the same day. You can always suggest a party once the pandemic restrictions have been lifted.

Conclusion

By now you will hopefully have a clearer idea of what a handfasting involves and some thoughts about the elements you might want to include in your own ceremony. You should also have a clearer idea of the types of ceremony and ritual that are available to you—something that can often be a bit bewildering, especially if you are a beginner pagan. At the end of the day, however, try not to worry too much. If you are a pagan, put your trust in the gods themselves that all will go as smoothly as possible. It is true, however, that the gods help those who help themselves, so do as much preparation as you feel you need to do, in good time, and most of all—have a wonderful day.

Chapter Six
Writing Your Vows

What's the most important thing that I tell handfastees?

Write your vows down!

You think you'll remember what you want to say—after all, these are words of commitment to the person you love most, which could bind you for a lifetime.

However, once you're actually in the ceremony, you may find that you're overcome with nerves or emotion. A lot of people cry. Sometimes your celebrants will cry! It's even worse if the words you've so lovingly crafted over the previous few weeks and have committed to memory like a professional actor simply drain out of your head.

Fortunately there's a simple answer: **write your vows down!** In this chapter, I will look at how to craft your own vows. I will give you some example formats, which you can build upon to create vows of your own. I will also give you some tips on delivering those vows.

If you have a piece of paper in front of you, even if it's just some notes as an *aide memoire*, it's a lot more reassuring—and no less heartfelt—in case you have to read your vows out.

You can make writing vows part of the handcrafting of your ceremony: use a special pen and a nice piece of parchment. If it looks good, it's a lovely thing to do, and you can perhaps put the copy into a pretty binder or an old leather-bound book to carry. I use a large leather- and gilt-bound blank book to hold the printout of the vows; it looks better than a scrap of A4. Not all celebrants follow this practice, however. Some prefer to learn a script.

We spoke to Dutch celebrant Henk Vis, whose practice is Druidic but who is also experienced in other traditions and has been arranging ceremonies for people for a number of years. He says,

> *I hate using snippets of paper or reading from a scroll. And take your time during [the] ceremony—there is no need for rush (I always think about the moment in church after the holy communion ... when the priest or vicar takes his time to clean up and fold and put away the cup and plate). When you are in the flow of the moment, the words will come.*

Make sure your celebrants have a printed copy of the vows as well. Then, if by chance you leave your vows sitting on the living room table, someone else will have a copy of them.

What Should I Say?

I encourage handfasting couples to write their own vows rather than using someone else's template (although you will find some suggestions in this chapter). It's more personal that way—part of the reason many folk choose a handfasting in the first place is that it's more personal and less of an official rote than a civil or church wedding, where the vows are pretty much set in stone in order to be legally binding.

But a lot of people don't want to write their own vows. Maybe they feel they can't write well enough, or that they really can't express what's in their hearts and souls. In this case, sometimes it really helps to have an idea—a hook to hang your own words upon, and that's why I give some examples.

Often, your vows are what you really want to say to your partner if no one was listening. It's like dancing when no one is watching! This can be intimidating—especially if you've only recently met your celebrants and your entire family and social circle are standing around. This is particularly pertinent to cultures that have a bit of a stiff upper lip—like the British. We'd rather make a joke of something than display our emotions so openly—but there's no reason why you can't include some humor in your vows. Making people laugh lightens the mood, and although a handfasting is meant to be a serious occasion, it doesn't have to be a solemn one, and it certainly doesn't need to be somber. Weddings aren't funerals, so don't treat them like one!

Some Sample Vows

Basically, the main thing on which you need to focus is what's in your heart. Don't be embarrassed to give voice to this—if not now, then when? Some people write poems, and some just say a sentence or two. Some handfastees prefer to "say" their vows silently, perhaps regarding their feelings as too private or sacred to be expressed in front of friends and family. That's fine, too! Remember, this is *your* handfasting. It's all about you, and whatever you decide to do, and however you express yourself. It is important only that your sentiments come from your heart and are uttered with sincerity. Even if you do so silently, the gods will still be able to hear you!

If you think you might need a prompt, let's look at some examples.

I call upon [god/goddess] to witness my vows to you. In the name of [god/goddess], may our love be acknowledged this day. You are my light and my life, and you have had my love ever since [date]. May the blessings of our love extend to the rest of our lives, and may we remain together as long as love shall last.

––––––

I remember when we first met [include some funny and happy memories here]. I knew you were the one for me when [the occasion]. I chose you because [your reasons]. [List your partner's qualities.]

––––––

Handfastee 1: Will you share my pain?
Handfastee 2: I will share it.
Handfastee 1: Will you share my laughter?
Handfastee 2: I will share it.
Handfastee 1: Will you share my burdens?

Handfastee 2: I will share them, and seek to ease them.

Handfastee 1: Will you share my dreams?

Handfastee 2: I will share them.

Handfastee 1: Will you honor me?

Handfastee 2: I will.

[Then reverse this so handfastee 2 is asking the questions.]

————

Handfastee 1: Will you promise to share my life as long as love shall last?

Handfastee 2: I will.

Handfastee 2: Will you promise to share my life as long as love shall last?

Handfastee 1: I will.

[Their hands are bound.]

————

Celebrant to handfastee 1: Do you promise to bind your life to [handfastee 2] for as long as you both shall desire it?

Handfastee 1: I do.

Celebrant to handfastee 2: Do you promise to bind your life to [handfastee 1] for as long as you both shall desire it?

Handfastee 2: I do.

Celebrant: Then shall your hands be bound, thus binding your hearts and lives together in the material world, for as long as love shall last.

————

Celebrant to handfastee 1: Repeat after me: I take [*handfastee 2*] to be my handfasted partner, in woe and weal, in sunlight and moonlight, in calm and storm. I wish our hands to be bound in honor of our vow.

[Handfastee 1 repeats this.]

Celebrant to handfastee 2: Repeat after me: I take [*handfastee 1*] to be my hand-fasted partner, in woe and weal, in sunlight and moonlight, in calm and storm. I wish our hands to be bound in honor of our vow.

[Handfastee 2 repeats this.]

Celebrant to handfastees: You have promised to be bound to one another. Do you now wish your hands to be bound?
Handfastees: We do.

[Celebrant binds their hands.]

Celebrant: Then may you both be bound in honor and love to one another.

―――

Celebrant to handfastee 1: This cord will bind you, symbolizing the love you have for one another. It is strong yet flexible, enduring yet yielding. Do you accept this binding as a representation of your love for [*handfastee 2*]?
Handfastee 1: I do.
Celebrant to handfastee 2: This cord will bind you, symbolizing the love you have for one another. It is strong yet flexible, enduring yet yielding. Do you accept this binding as a representation of your love for [*handfastee 1*]?
Handfastee 2: I do.
Celebrant: Then may your hands be bound just as your souls are entwined with your love for one another.

[Celebrant binds their hands.]

―――

Celebrant to handfastees: Your hands are about to be bound with this cord. These are the hands that clasp one another. These are hands that wipe away tears, that come together in a clap of joy. These are hands that care for your children, that bake and make and heal and hold. These are the hands that will be bound together. Do you wish to make these hands fast?
Handfastees: We do.

———

If you want many different ideas for handfasting vows and rituals, you might like to check out Raven Kaldera and Tannin Schwartzstein's *Inviting Hera's Blessing: Handfasting and Wedding Rituals*. They include a large number of rituals for combined religions, as well as for different types of handfasting, and their book is an invaluable resource.

Reincarnation

Some people choose to include the idea that they will be bound in the reincarnation cycle by the handfasting. It is up to you whether this is a good idea or not, or whether to leave it up to the powers that be.

Conclusion

Your vows are central to the handfasting ceremony, and it can be a daunting task to both write your vows and speak them out loud. As a celebrant, I would say that this is one of the aspects of handfasting that gives handfastees the most trouble. Use some of the examples above as a template or check online for ideas. Your vows should come from your heart and, above all, be sincere. This is your chance to really express your love for, and commitment to, your partner, in a way that is more personal and individual than the rote vows you might speak in a legally binding wedding ceremony.

Chapter Seven
What You Will Need

Modern pagans often use specific tools in rituals in order to honor the elements with which we work. Some of these—the chalice, the athame or ritual knife—have become classic symbols of the various pagan paths, just as there are symbols of marriage itself. The wedding ring is one of these, for example. We might note that some of the symbols of handfasting have passed into common sayings around marriage: we've mentioned "tying the knot" and "jumping the broomstick." You may want to include an actual broomstick in your own ceremony. You might also want to include some of the tools of the pagan repertoire, too. In this chapter, we will be taking a look at some of these tools.

Your celebrant will bring everything they need in order to conduct your handfasting, so it should not be necessary for you to make or bring any of your own ritual tools, such as a chalice or a wand—but you may want to do so. You can discuss this with your celebrant beforehand to avoid any confusion. We usually ask people if they are intending to supply their own handfasting cord, for example.

In many pagan paths, such as Wicca or Druidry, we work on a fourfold system of symbols based on the four elements. Ritual tools correlate to each element. If you work within paganism already, you'll be familiar with these, but if you do not, they are earth, air, fire, and water.

Each element has a ritual tool attached to it:

- Earth: A pentacle or stone
- Air: A sword (a wand in some traditions)
- Fire: A wand (conversely, a sword in some traditions)
- Water: A cup or chalice

And each element is associated with a direction:

- Earth: North
- Air: East
- Fire: South
- Water: West

These symbols form the four cornerstones of many pagan rituals, including many handfastings. These four magical tools correspond to four "weapons" of significance in Celtic myth—the sword, the spear, the shield, and the cauldron (and/or grail). The same four ritual tools also appear in the magical practices of the Western Hermetic tradition, derived from the Golden Dawn, and they appear in tarot decks as the four card suits: swords, cups, wands, and pentacles.

If you would like to use these in your own handfasting ceremony, you may want to bring, for example, a wand crafted for your handfasting, your own athame, a loving cup or chalice, or handfasting cord or ribbon.

I will take a look first at tools for your handfasting altar, and then at other ritual elements, such as your handfasting cord and wedding rings.

The Altar

Most magical practitioners work with an altar, and many handfastings will include one, but this depends where your ceremony is held: if indoors, you or your celebrant might set up a more ornate altar, which nonetheless may be temporary; outdoors will depend on what's available.

If I'm conducting a handfasting in a stone circle, such as Stanton Drew near Bristol, which has a number of flat stones, I'll use a flat stone as an altar. I have learned through painful experience not to balance a chalice full of water on an uneven rock, however, so whether you are celebrant or hand-fastee, be careful where you put things, and be especially careful about heat. A handy tree stump might also be an option, otherwise a rudimentary altar can be set up on the ground. You do not have to have an altar at your hand-fasting, however; many people choose not to have one.

As with most other aspects of the craft, there is no single "right" way to build an altar—indeed, it is a wonderfully individual thing. Some of us have altars crowded with many statues of gods and goddesses. Some people prefer to have seasonal greenery—snowdrops, primroses, hawthorn, or autumn leaves—on their altar. Many altars are very abstract. I've known ones that feature action figures and cartoon cats! It all depends on your own preferences.

Most people use a large box or a small table for their altar. You can get very elaborate, specially made altars, but these are not necessary, especially if you are intending to bring your altar to the handfasting site. Ideally, the top of the altar should be about waist height, as this is easiest for working.

Tools on the Altar

Your handfasting altar might, for instance, hold photos of yourself and your beloved, or the rings, or the handfasting cord. A basic altar, however, holds the following:

- Your wand (if you have one)
- A cup or chalice
- An athame or knife
- Pentacles
- An incense holder
- As many candles as you like (and as many as are safe)
- A small dish of earth or a stone or crystal (anything that symbolizes earth)

Some people prefer to have a cloth on their altar (practically, this is in case your candles overflow), but although useful and pleasant, it is not essential.

Wands

Some handfasting couples choose to make a wand for their ceremony, perhaps in a wood designated by one of the Ogham systems that correlates to the month in which your handfasting is held. The wand is used to draw the circle at the start of the handfasting ceremony, but some couples also like to use the wand as a ring holder.

The Celtic tree calendar, or Ogham, is a system of correspondences that connects the trees to months of the year. Please bear in mind that the ancient Celts themselves almost certainly had a different system (likely to be lunar), and this is a modern equivalent (you will come across different variations of the tree calendar, which link different trees to different months).

Once you've chosen your tree, go out and find one. It is advisable to "ask" the tree if it is acceptable to cut a wand from it. Your wand should be about the length of your arm from elbow to fingertip. You can either strip the bark from it and leave it to dry or leave the bark on it.

You can also buy wands of varying types (not just wooden, but metal and other materials) from your local or online occult shop.

Cup or Chalice

A chalice (from the Latin *calix*, "mug," borrowed from ancient Greek *kalyx*, "shell" or "husk") is a goblet or footed cup intended to hold a drink. The ancient Roman *calix* was a drinking vessel consisting of a bowl fixed on top of a stand, and it was used in Roman banquets. In general religious terms, a chalice is intended for drinking during a ceremony. Handfasting couples often use a chalice, sometimes a double-sided one, to drink during the nuptials: a sip of wine as a toast to one another's health, for example.

Unless you are a fairly experienced woodturner, making your own wooden chalice probably isn't going to be an option, but you can commission one from a local craftsman. My partner made a Saxon-inspired Wassail cup for a customer, who was going to give it to her parents as a wedding anniversary present. It had their names inscribed on it, and they loved it.

Occult shops usually have a good range of chalices, and there are also options online, but you can scour the secondhand shops as well for antique glass. For a time, our shop hosted the occultist Dion Fortune's chalice. It was a big wine glass, dark green and made in the style of Portuguese "beco" ware (so called because the pattern on it looks like rows of little birds' beaks). It probably dates from the 1930s, and I think Dion Fortune picked it up in a junk or homeware shop—it certainly wasn't intended to be used as a chalice, but it made a good one, all the same. I use one that was given to my mother by her father; it is a small wooden cup that was made from the wood of a beam in Coventry Cathedral after the building was bombed in the Second World War. It certainly wasn't intended for use as a chalice in pagan ceremonies—but this is what it has become.

Athame

The athame (often pronounced *ath-ahmay* or *athayme*) is mentioned in the writings of Gerald Gardner in the 1950s, who claimed to have been initiated into a surviving tradition of witchcraft: the New Forest Coven in Hampshire, England (evidence suggests they were a combination of Theosophists, members of the Golden Dawn and Co-Masonry, and other esoteric traditions). The athame was their foremost ritual tool and is now one of the four elemental tools in Wicca traditionally representing fire, as does the ritual sword. In a handfasting ceremony, the athame can be used to draw the initial circle instead of a wand.

The athame is an individual ritual tool, while the sword is more appropriate as a coven tool or the personal tool of the High Priest or High Priestess. There are obvious risks associated with an entire group of people all wielding swords while confined within a small ritual circle space nine feet in diameter; this safety factor, as well as ease of use, may explain why the emphasis within Wicca is more on each witch's personal athame rather than the ritual sword.

The athame's primary function in ritual work or spell work is to channel and direct psychic energy, usually conceived of as a kind of etheric fire, and you can use it to draw your handfasting circle.

You do not have to make your own athame—unless you are an experienced blacksmith! You can buy one online or from your local occult shop (old-school Wiccans may tell you that you must be given an athame rather than buy it yourself, but many pagans do not adhere to this view—on the other hand, you might like to ask someone close to buy it for you as a handfasting gift!). Quality athames can be quite expensive, and it is not necessary to have one at your handfasting. It is not, in fact, necessary to have any ritual tool—but it is nice. You can sometimes find suitable knives secondhand; some people use ornamental paper knives, and I use a *sgian dhu* found in a vintage military shop.

Pentacles

Some people just use a stone or crystal for the northern quarter of their handfasting circle, since it represents earth. Others like to use a representation of a pentacle. If you are good at pyrography (etching onto wood with a hot pen like a small soldering iron), you may like to have a go at reproducing a pentacle or pentagram onto a circle of wood. You can buy them, too, made out of wood, pewter, or other metals or stained glass. Or, if you're into embroidery, you can embroider one and hang it in the northern station. A pentacle is a symbol that is part of the decoration of the handfasting circle, and you don't actually need to do anything with it, although you might like to place your rings and handfasting cord upon it.

Candles

Generally, pagan ceremonies use a main altar candle, often natural wax or white, along with four candles for each quarter. Colors vary according to different traditions, but a standard practice is as follows:

- East: Yellow/white
- South: Red/orange
- West: Blue
- North: Black/green

You don't have to follow this in your handfasting, however, and be aware of practicalities: if your ceremony is outside, it is advisable to have your candles in lantern holders, especially if it's windy.

If you are working with a particular god or goddess, you might also like to choose a candle that is of a color that is sacred to that particular deity.

Your Handfasting Cord

The handfasting cord symbolizes the union of the couple. It is what is meant by "tying the knot," and it represents the love that binds two people together. It is not an essential part of a handfasting; your celebrant can simply place your hands together. Most people, however, choose to use a handfasting cord within the ceremony as a symbol of their love.

A lot of handfasting couples prefer to make their own cords. If you are experienced in braiding, you can make your own with the aid of a "bobbin." Or you can buy lengths of colored cord (dressing gown cord is unromantic but practical) and braid them together in a plait. As with other ritual tools, you can also buy handfasting cords online or from your local witchcraft shop.

Colors for the Cord

What colors should you choose for your handfasting cord? This depends on the symbolism you are intending to produce:

Pink: The traditional color of love in contemporary Western societies, but some people feel that it's a bit too stereotyped. But if you like it, have it!

Red: Devotees of Thelemic entities, such as Babalon, might like red, and it can look stunning as a bridal gown, too. It can represent lust rather than love, but it also evokes fire and flame. It is a popular color among brides in Mexico.

Green: I've seen a number of green bridal gowns and cords, particularly among Druids and pagans who are following a nature-based path. The days in which green was regarded as unlucky as a wedding color are more or less gone—it's a positive color for pagans, not an unlucky one.

Blue: We always think of white as symbolizing purity and chastity, but in fact this only dates from Victorian times. Prior to that, blue, the color of the Virgin Mary, was regarded in many countries as the color of purity.

White: Traditional wedding dresses are white, but this does not date from ancient times. White's popularity really only dates from 1840, which was when Queen Victoria married Prince Albert in a white gown trimmed with Honiton lace. Brides rushed to copy the Queen, and eventually white became standardized. But Victoria wasn't the first: Princess Philippa of England was married in white (with an ermine trim) as far back as 1406, and in 1559, Mary, Queen of Scots, also wore white for her first wedding. But these women were unusual: many colors were popular for wedding dresses up until the Victorian era, and black was particularly popular in Scandinavia—a trend revived by Goths! White remains popular as a choice for handfasting cords, echoing the white dresses of many brides.

Purple: A popular choice among witches! I've seen a number of purple and green handfasting cords and countless purple wedding gowns.

Silver or Gold: Metallic cord can look stunning.

Black: A popular choice for a Gothic wedding, and why not? There's no reason why you shouldn't have a black wedding dress, either.

One of the things to remember about a handfasting cord is that this is often something you might want to keep. I know quite a few handfasting couples who chose to keep the handfasting cord for display—for example, wrapped around the handle of the broomstick over which they jumped at the end of the ceremony. This is a lovely thing to do, and you may therefore choose to make the cord as pretty as possible.

Further Color Symbolism for Cords

Red: Fertility, passion, strength, courage, health, vigor
Festival: Yule
Planet: Mars
Day: Tuesday
Astrological Sign: Scorpio

Orange: Encouragement, adaptability, stimulation, attraction, plenty, kindness

Festival: Candlemas

Deity: Brigit

Planets: Sun, Mercury

Days: Sunday, Tuesday, Wednesday

Yellow: Attraction, charm, confidence, balance, harmony, knowledge, learning, concentration, persuasion, joy, comfort

Planet: Mercury

Day: Wednesday

Astrological Signs: Gemini, Leo

Deity: Mercury

Green: Finances, fertility, luck, success, charity, growth, rejuvenation, prosperity, nurturing, beauty, health, ambition, counteracting greed and jealousy

Planets: Venus, Mercury

Days: Friday, Wednesday

Festivals: Spring equinox, Beltane

Astrological Sign: Taurus

Deities: Persephone, Hestia

Blue: Tranquility, understanding, patience, health, truth, devotion, sincerity, honor, loyalty, peace, wisdom, protection during sleep, astral projection

Light Blue: Understanding, patience, health

Dark Blue: A safe journey, longevity, strength

Planets: Moon, Venus, Saturn, Jupiter

Days: Monday, Friday, Saturday, Thursday

Astrological Signs: Libra, Sagittarius

Purple: Power, piety, sanctity, sentimentality, tension, sadness, amplification of other energies, wisdom, high ideals, spiritual protection and healing, psychic ability, protective energy, strength, progress

Planet: Jupiter

Day: Thursday

Astrological Sign: Sagittarius

Pink: Unity, honor, truth, romance, happiness, healing, familial or
emotional love (rather than sexual), friendship, affections, unselfish
emotions, spiritual healing, banishing hatred

Gem: Rose quartz

Planet: Venus

Day: Friday

But there is a deeper magic to handfasting cords.

Cord magic is part of old-school Wicca, and there's a lot of magical symbolism behind its use. The whole idea of handfasting itself is bound up in that symbolism: the idea that by binding hands, you bind souls and hearts. If you watched the royal wedding between Prince William and Kate Middleton, you may have noticed an element familiar to many pagans partway through: the couple's hands were wrapped briefly in a yellow cloth by the Archbishop of Canterbury. Their wedding was a mainstream, if lavish, Christian ceremony, but the old idea of bound hands was nonetheless incorporated.

In ancient Roman ceremonies, the bride would wear a "bride's belt," called the *Nodus Herculaneus* after the knotted belt of Hercules. It was intended to symbolize virility, since Hercules is said to have fathered no fewer than seventy children. The belt is tied in such a way that only the groom can (hopefully!) loosen it once the couple are in bed together. Some people believe that this is another origin of the phrase "tying the knot," although the bride and her helpers tie the original knot in this instance, and the groom unties it.

The cord itself has a long history. We can include some other, newer elements: one of our handfasting couples introduced us to the idea of passing a bowl of little ribbons around the congregation. Each person takes one and holds it for a few minutes, perhaps as the couple say their vows, and mentally put their good wishes into the little ribbons. Then they tie the ribbons onto the main handfasting cord, which is also handed around at the same time.

Paul Cudby, whom we met in previous chapters, says,

Having all our loved ones using ribbons blessed by Simon [the celebrant] to tie our hands together [was]…a reminder of the part that everyone plays in the developing relationship. Two people are made one not just by their own actions but by the encouragement and support of those around them.

If you have small children involved—and if you trust them!—you or your celebrant can send them around with the bowl of ribbons. It's an easy thing for them to do and makes them feel important, so small bridesmaids or pages can be entrusted with this task. The adults can handle passing the cord around themselves. If you time it properly (and people are usually sensible enough not to hang on to the cord for ages), you can arrange matters so that the beribboned handfasting cord reaches the end of the circle just as the couple are about to finish their vows—just in time for the actual handfasting.

This is a lovely thing to do and, importantly, makes everyone feel involved in the ceremony in a way that they can understand, which can be an issue with nonpagan congregations. It's inclusive, and the results, in the form of the beribboned handfasting cord, are very pretty.

The Ring

Although the focus of the handfasting ceremony is often seen as the handfasting cord, to many couples raised with the traditional idea of marriage, the ring is often equally important.

Rings can take many forms. We have a historical record of one ceremony in which the ring was lost (a best man's worst nightmare), so a witness "stooped down and made a ring of a rush, and would have given it them."[26] Elizabethan and other accounts can be quite specific about the wedding ring: "A seal ring of gold with the picture of a white dog upon it, with the ears tipped with silver."[27] Hoop rings were mentioned, and some styles were popular, such as the double-hooped "gimmel" ring—a double ring that twists apart to become two linked rings, symbolizing clasped hands. The Museum of London has a gold gimmel ring of circa 1600, engraved with a posy and a handfasting motto:

26. Nicholl, "The Lodger Shakespeare."
27. Nicholl, "The Lodger Shakespeare."

As handes doe shut

So hart [heart] be knit

Some rings incorporated "memento mori" devices—reminders of death, popular with the Elizabethans—to remind the wearer the marriage was until death should part them from their beloved.

Couples also exchanged a piece or coin made of gold, broken in half to symbolize two hearts that could be united as one. And we have records of other betrothal gifts: a pair of gloves "worth 2s 6d," a petticoat, a "peece of crimson rybbyn knitt in a square knott wch she called a treww lovers knott," a "jewell called an aggat," a prayer book, and "a French crowne and a tothepiker [toothpick] of silver."[28]

I know couples who (if they have experience in silversmithing, for example) have made their own rings, or who have commissioned them with a pagan design from jewelers. You can buy ready-made rings, too: one popular ring bears an inscription in Elvish (no, not *that* one, although the design is obviously based on the ring in *Lord of the Rings*). Some people also choose to have a ring that is not explicitly pagan but that they just happen to like—and why not? As with all other aspects of handfasting, it's your ceremony.

Some historical accounts suggest that the ring was worn on the third finger of the left hand—as it still is today in a number of countries—because the Romans believed that a nerve ran from this finger up to the heart. This may align with ancient ideas about energy currents, but with many people's familiarity with concepts such as shiatsu meridians, the idea is not an entirely alien one.

Not everyone likes rings or is able to wear them; they're not essential. I have done many ceremonies in which the couple have not wanted a ring and concentrated instead on the handfasting cord. Some people choose to exchange necklaces instead.

---

28. Nicholl, "The Lodger Shakespeare."

Conclusion

You do not have to use any of these ritual elements—the four tools, a ring, or a cord—in your handfasting ceremony. The ritual can simply consist of yourselves, your celebrants, and your joined hands and spoken vows. It depends purely on how elaborate you want your ceremony to be—but if you want to include some of these pagan elements, you are free to do so. Incorporate some of the classic symbols of paganism into your handfasting and show your guests what it's all about.

Chapter Eight

Etiquette, Ethics, and When Things Go Wrong

In this chapter, we will discuss the etiquette involved in handfasting: popping the question, invitations, dealing with difficult guests, and troubleshooting when something—gods forbid—goes wrong at your ceremony. It is wise to expect that *something* will go wrong, but with a little forethought, you can reduce the risk factor! I'll be suggesting some ways to sort out any difficult issues early on.

I remember, with some wincing, a ceremony I officiated on the slopes of Glastonbury Tor. We had all assembled to walk up the hill; the bride was there, the groom was there, I had all the ritual tools, the weather was brilliantly sunny after a day of rain, and I was just congratulating myself on getting all this together when I turned, trod on a patch of slippery mud, and fell flat on my face. Pretending I was not covered in mud—I had it in my *hair*—to retain some semblance of dignity was not an easy task. Fortunately, pagans tend to be both highly pragmatic and have a sense of humor, and the couple were more concerned that their priestess was all right rather than worrying about the fact that she was suddenly covered in filth. However, it was a salutary lesson from the gods that if you are going to undertake rituals outside, you need to be prepared for all eventualities.

This is a section for both celebrants (we'll include some tips for you) and handfastees—remember, you're all in this together! Helen Woodsford-Dean mentions that people often fail to think things through—don't be one of these people! Your celebrant can only help you up to a point. As Helen says,

> *With ten years' experience, we've gotten better at anticipating problems and picking up when a potential issue may arise so we can head it off. Less problems now than in the beginning, and that's down to experience. We've also gotten better at suggesting alternatives or just saying no—to the point of honoring ourselves and stating, "Sorry, we are not the best celebrants for you ..."*

Proposals

Let's start from the very beginning: popping the question. Asking someone to marry you has got to be one of the most nerve-wracking questions you will ever ask in your life, and the nature of the proposal can be fraught. I think it is fair to say that most people do prefer a romantic proposal into which some thought has been placed. I don't think it matters these days who proposes to whom—women don't have to wait four years until a leap year to pop the question. But a little bit of care really is essential.

I was recently listening to presenter Graham Norton's radio show on BBC Radio 2, and listeners started writing in about the proposals they'd had. One man proposed quite casually as he was sitting with his girlfriend on the sofa watching *Homes under the Hammer*. He didn't take his eyes off the screen, and although she said yes (she had been waiting for him to propose for four years), the actual moment didn't have an enormous amount of glamor, let's say. Another listener wrote in to say that her boyfriend had proposed to her in a motorway service station. If you are going to propose, you don't necessarily have to go down on one knee with a ring and a bunch of flowers—but a little thought would not go amiss!

Remember, too, the story of "how X proposed to me" is going to be told and retold among family and friends. If you want some happy memories, then a well-crafted or romantic proposal is a must. This might sound ridiculous, but practicing in front of a mirror is not a bad plan. If you're proposing with a ring, make sure you have remembered to bring it with you! Proposals in front of an audience are fraught with hazard. I once was witness to one of these in, of all places, a restaurant in Siberia: a young man sitting behind us suddenly went down on one knee, produced a ring as a florist came in with an enormous bunch of roses, and proposed. Fortunately, the young woman said yes…but what if your partner doesn't? And the bigger the audience, the bigger the risk. Do you really want to be rejected in front of the entire Superbowl?

Try not to propose with gimmicks. Men's magazine *GQ*, for instance, suggests you don't try anything ambitious, such as attaching the ring to your beloved dog's collar and sending him to your partner.[29] What could possibly go wrong? *GQ* refers to proposals as "too big with the ask"—or too small. Too big (popping the question as you're skydiving, for instance) and you risk it going wrong, and too small—well, the service station example is a good one. You want the proposal to be a little bit memorable.

Wedding experts also suggest you don't propose on a significant holiday— like Valentine's Day. If you get turned down, it associates the day with some sad or bitter memories, and that's a shame, so a neutral day that doesn't have significance for you is best. And if the person says yes, you have another date with happy memories attached!

Timing is important—it's a good plan to propose if you have already discussed the possibility of marriage. Not, for instance, when you've only known someone for a couple of weeks.

Also, in a poll taken by online wedding magazine *The Knot* of the main proposal faux pas, top of the list was "proposing without a ring."[30] In general, people seem to like some tangible evidence of the proposal—even if it's a temporary ring made of wildflowers, for example.

If you really get stuck, google "marriage proposal idea generator" (seriously).

29. Justin Myers, "How to Propose," accessed November 3, 2020, https://www
.gq-magazine.co.uk/lifestyle/article/how-to-propose.

30. Simone Hill, "66 Proposal Ideas to Spark Romance," *The Knot*, accessed November
3, 2020, https://www.theknot.com/content/romantic-ways-to-propose.

Reassuring Your Guests

Taking part in a handfasting can be a rather unsettling experience for your guests if they are not pagans and if they have not taken part in a ritual before. In Western culture, most people have been to a church at some point in their lives, quite often for a wedding, and they know roughly what is expected of them and how to behave. But a handfasting—a pagan ritual—is entirely different territory. Many people, even if they are your relatives, are only familiar with the notion of paganism, if at all, from the media, and as we all know, that tends to be pretty sensationalist. Expect actual trepidation from some of your more sensitive connections and, as mentioned earlier, jokes about goat sacrifice from the more robust ones. Basically, people won't know what to do, and lack of confidence leads to nerves. However, there are lots of ways in which you can minimize this.

In practice, particularly if your ritual contains mention of the four directions, most people really enjoy handfastings. As also mentioned, handfasting is paganism's "shopwindow"—the introduction that most nonpagans have to the various paths of paganism and their practices. Most people understand the idea of the four directions, and they like it. It's a familiar and therefore reassuring aspect to them.

I tend to give a brief introduction to the ceremony and try to be reassuring—jokes are all very well, but a nervous congregation can be a nightmare, and there is absolutely no point in making people more anxious. I therefore say something like the following before undertaking the sort of ceremony we looked at in chapter 5:

Welcome everyone to [name] and [name's] handfasting. This is an old form of wedding ceremony, from the time of the Celts and the Saxons, and you'll find some familiar elements here, such as "tying the knot"—this is where that expression comes from! And so does "jumping the broomstick." Before we get to the handfasting itself, we're going to inscribe a circle in the air—in a church, we're already in a sacred space, but here in [wherever it is], we need to make a sacred space for ourselves, and this is how we do it.

I'm going to walk around you in a circle, with this wand, and I'm going to "draw" a circle in the air. As I do this, imagine a circle of white light around us: that's our sacred space.

Then we're going to take a "sacred day" for ourselves, starting in the east, by invoking the rising of the sun, and moving south to noon, then west to the evening, and north to midnight. This makes our sacred day for the duration of the handfasting, and when we come to the end of the ceremony, we'll "undo" it all.

If you'd like to let your guests know a little bit about this process in advance, print the information out in a nice font and circulate it to them.

Having said all this, most people who are actually prepared to attend a pagan ceremony are usually curious (rather than alarmed) and prepared to have an intriguing time.

"Interesting" People

I take the title of this section from the late great actor Alan Rickman, who was once asked why he chose to play villains so often. Looking down his nose, Rickman replied something along the lines of, "I don't play villains. I play … interesting … people."

What happens if you do have a guest who reacts badly?

In practice, I've never had a problem with a guest at a ceremony that Trevor and myself have jointly conducted. Trevor, operating on his own as a celebrant, had the aunt of one bride (a fundamentalist Christian) make a fuss loudly during a ceremony. He stopped her and told her she was not going to be allowed to disrupt or divert the ceremony, that she should simply leave and be embarrassed that she had let herself down in front of her family—which got a small round of applause. The bride never spoke to her aunt again. I've also had one instance of a fundamentalist relative refusing to attend; the attitude of the couple in that case was "good riddance." Personally, I have never known anyone to show up with the intention of causing trouble, but if this does happen, your best bet is to get rid of them as quickly as possible. It is highly probable, however, that as a handfasting couple, you will have some idea of which of your connections is likely to cause problems. In that case, the answer is simple: don't invite them. It is easier to deal with an affronted relation than to wrestle someone out of a ceremony after they've already spoiled it.

If you disinvite someone, tell them the truth: you did not invite them because you thought they were likely to be offended, and you didn't want the risk of them causing a scene at the ceremony. If *that* offends them, tough. It is your ceremony, your sacred and meaningful day, and you are entitled to draw boundaries and not have that day hijacked by someone else's religious agenda. Helen Woodsford-Dean counsels,

> *Then there are the "interfaith" weddings where the guests are fundamentalists and think we are Satanists. We've got really good over the years at mitigating for this and toning down any overly "strong" Pagan references, and we have had staunch Christians telling us afterward how beautiful it was ("even though hell awaits").*

Stick to your guns and be firm, especially if you have a very fundamentalist family. In which case, perhaps don't tell them at all. Have your beautiful ceremony with people who know what's going on and who appreciate it. Ironically, Covid's impact on wedding ceremonies means that this process has been made slightly simpler, as there could be restrictions on the numbers of guests.

Questions after the Ceremony

Once your guests have gone through your handfasting ceremony, they may have questions afterward, either for you or for your celebrant. Quite often after a handfasting, I am approached by friends or relatives who "want to know what it's all about." And unfortunately, I can usually predict the reaction of one of these connections—he's usually a man—when I start explaining that this is an old traditional ceremony based on Celtic or Saxon practices. There will be a brief pause as the guest digests this information, and then he will start feeling around the boundaries of ideology, making comments about how nice it is to have a British or an English ceremony.

Since it's undeniably the case that handfastings do, in some form, stem from historical customs in the British Isles, as we saw in chapter 1, you aren't going to be in a position to directly refute this—nor should you. However, you should also be aware that, although the guest sometimes just leaves it at that, your agreement that it is a British ceremony can sometimes open the door to an avowal of actual nationalism, and these days, this is not always a good thing, especially when it leads into a soapbox rant about "other people" coming over "here" with their foreign ways.

I usually deal with this by steering the conversation in another direction, and I sometimes say something along the lines of, "Of course, other peoples' traditions are also perfectly valid, and there can be some really lovely ceremonies that are held in other countries." Unless the person is going to look totally churlish, this statement is anodyne enough for them to agree with while flagging that you yourself don't want to go down the path of agreeing with horrendous racism.

Thus, I am sometimes the UKIP (UK Independence Party) whisperer at handfastings. The couple are usually aware of Uncle Fred's dodgy political opinions and may well have banned him from venting them or are otherwise keeping an eye on him. I feel, however, that it is my job as a celebrant to pour what oil I may on any troubled waters rather than stirring them with a big spoon—and usually the guest themself goes away, happy that they have witnessed something "traditional." This may be a bit annoying to the celebrant—but then again, it's not their big day.

The Benefit of Ushers

Cat Pentaberry, whom we met in an earlier chapter, is another experienced celebrant who also counsels people to think of every little detail. For example,

I would have made sure we had someone to open the door for our guests. The friend I asked to do this arrived late and the job fell to my partner, who as bridegroom felt rather stressed by it.

You might want to consider enlisting a friend as an usher, just as you would for a more conventional wedding, especially if it's a large and perhaps complex ceremony with many guests. Your celebrant might take this role if it's a small handfasting, but their focus should really be on the handfasting couple and the magic and ritual underpinning the ceremony, not on directing the guests.

Cameras

Handfastees often ask if photographs are allowed. I reply that this is always up to the couple. While many pagans—particularly older ones—are reluctant to allow photography in an actual ritual, a handfasting can often be the exception to this. It is a semipublic ceremony, often with nonpagans present, and it really is down to the couple if they want a video or photographic record of the ceremony itself. However, I advise that this should be discreet and should not disrupt the ritual aspects of the handfasting. Helen Woodsford-Dean adds that, in her experience,

> …*sometimes the wedding "professionals" are a problem, like the photographer who shouted out (after the couple jumped the broomstick) "I didn't catch that, can you do it again?" Now we tell them that we don't want to know they are there. A professional should be unobtrusive; that's what a zoom lens is for.*

However, check it out with your guests if you have any doubts, both about photographs being taken in the first place and also with regard to photos being put online, especially if people are tagged in them. Some pagans, particularly those in professional positions such as teaching, nursing, or law enforcement, may not be happy about being "outed" on social media. This attitude is changing as paganism slowly becomes more mainstream, especially in the UK, but people's religious privacy must still be respected as it can cause serious problems for them in their professional lives.

Handfastings often do not have the budget of weddings, and a professional photographer can cost a lot. Most of the handfastings I have done did not, in fact, have a professional wedding photographer in attendance and relied on photos taken by a family member or friend with an interest in photography.

As with other professionals who may be involved in your handfasting, if you do hire a photographer, it is important to feel comfortable with them and to check out references and testimonials. Anyone can assemble an impressive social media page or website using images that someone else has taken; make sure you hire someone reputable who has a verifiable track record. Word of mouth is a good way of finding a suitable person. Most professional wedding photographers will be happy to furnish their credentials and samples of their work. They are not shy of charging, either: expect to part with a three-figure sum. It is a good idea to sign a contract with anyone you bring in to do your photography.

However, you are likely to be happier with the result if you go down the professional route, and if you do regard your handfasting as a lifetime commitment, you will want a record of your day that brings back memories, not something that you wince upon revisiting.

If you ask a friend or relative to do your photography, I suggest you make sure there is a backup person to step in, as well. For some reason, it is often this aspect of the handfasting that goes awry.

Phones

Nothing ruins a romantic, mystical atmosphere as much as a mobile phone suddenly shrilling out or randomly beeping. Celebrants have learned the hard way to insist that phones should be switched off or put on vibrate at the beginning of the ceremony, even if your guests want to take snaps on their mobiles.

Running Late

It's always a bit of a nightmare when things don't run on schedule—and weddings seem particularly prone to delays. I once had to hold up a handfasting for two hours because some of the quarter officers were stuck on the motorway, and another one because the bride was doing—well, I'm not sure what she was doing, but it took three hours, whatever it was. Fortunately (sort of), the handfasting was in her back garden, but I have found that it is as well not to have back-to-back handfastings on the same day if it can possibly be avoided. As a pagan celebrant, unlike a vicar or priest, I usually have the luxury of doing this and have basically adopted the practice of setting aside the whole day to devote to the handfasting. If not—and this has sometimes happened on the big festivals, such as a year when two couples wanted their handfasting on the winter solstice itself—Trevor and I have divided and conquered and done separate ceremonies individually.

The only wedding I have cut fine in terms of time was my stepson's, and we were not the celebrants. It was a big country manor wedding and we had lunch in a pub (in our own county) literally fifteen minutes from the venue. We had a map in the car and had downloaded instructions from Google Earth … which took us to the back gate of the several-hundred-acre property, and for reasons of the English landscape, it proved impossible to find the front gate. You'd think you could just go around the perimeter … anyway, having driven across half of Somerset and getting hotter and crosser, we missed the ceremony entirely and arrived just as the happy couple were signing the register.

This is obviously not ideal. It's much better to leave plenty of time—particularly if you are officiating and the handfasting can't start without you. And, depending on the location, one of the problems with starting late is that your guests sometimes don't have enough to do with themselves except go to the bar …

How Long Should a Handfasting Take?

This will depend, obviously, on the complexity of the ceremony. However, the circle/consecration/quarter calling opening, the body of the ritual, and the closing usually take about half an hour to forty-five minutes. I would be reluctant to let the ceremony run for more than an hour, especially if people are expected to stand. Have pity on your poor guests, particularly if they are disabled and/or elderly and if it is cold or hot! Helen Johnson at Life Rites told me about one of her more challenging experiences:

A New York actress, who was having a handfasting in a castle near Edin-
burgh, had written and stage blocked the whole ceremony for me—it was
1.5 hours long and very theatrical. It took a little persuading for me to edit
(and rewrite) in order to crop it down to thirty minutes, which was perfectly
beautiful for the occasion. She had three outfit changes written into the orig-
inal script. Mind you, she had three separate handfastings in three different
countries!

Children and Your Handfasting

"Never work with children and animals!" While you may have a sneaking
sympathy with this view, you may also feel that handfastings are an ideal celebration to which to invite children. It is a happy day, often quite an informal
one (unlike a big, structured church wedding), and if it is outside, there is a
lot of opportunity for children to run around and enjoy themselves (weather
permitting!). Because you can arrange your ceremony yourself, this also gives
you the chance to give the kids something to do.

With traditional church weddings, children's roles are limited. Maybe
a small number will be allowed to be bridesmaids or page boys, but on the
whole they are expected to dress up, behave themselves, and keep quiet; they
may also have to sit still for a long time. Not so with a handfasting! Although
they are expected to behave themselves, there is usually more opportunity
to let off steam. Children can be naturally responsible and enjoy being given
responsibilities, too. It is also nice to include everyone if you are blending a
family—participation brings people together. Cat in Germany advises,

If you have several children as guests, plan for their needs: entertainment,
snacks, someone to look after them, and some space set aside for them.

Children usually enjoy the relaxed, often outdoor atmosphere of a handfasting and like the chance to dress up, but—especially if you are the bride—
you may not want to be distracted by small tearful people in the middle of
your ceremony, so it's crucial that someone else has that responsibility, at
least for a few hours. As Helen Woodsford-Dean says,

Couples with children are always more focused on the children than on the ceremony. Likewise, pets. Best to have a child/pet minder present.

Give kids something to do, therefore:

Hand around ribbons to tie to the handfasting cord

Hand around flowers

Attend you as bridesmaid/page boy

Ask them to read a little poem

Older children can be given more complex things to do. I officiated at a handfasting where the bride's daughter sang a stunningly atmospheric version of "She Moved Through the Fair."

Teenagers are legendary for finding anything done by their parents to be ridiculous and also for being hideously self-conscious, so make sure they're comfortable with anything you ask them to do (enlisting them as an unofficial backup photographer, for instance).

Don't forget to mention your children during the ceremony: you might like to thank them by name, for example, or give them a little gift, perhaps after you have said your vows. Again, this makes everyone feel included and brings them into this new chapter on which you are embarking.

Speeches

This is another aspect of the handfasting or wedding that is often fraught with hazard: the cliché of the groom's best friend, somewhat the worse for drink, making rambling, off-color remarks has a basis in fact! Unfortunately. Check with your guests (such as the bride's father or the best man) as to what they're likely to say, and make it clear if there are any subjects that are off-limits. Make it clear if you'd prefer there to be a time limit on their speech. It's easier to sort this out before the ceremony or reception than once someone has launched into their long, rambling monologue.

Don't be too attached to the format of your handfasting. It's not quite the same as a wedding—and there's nothing to say that you shouldn't change the format of an actual wedding, either. You might, for instance, want to ask your High Priest/Priestess to give a speech or say grace before the reception meal.

Rehearsals

Do you want to rehearse the handfasting? In general, most of our handfast-ees don't bother with a rehearsal, although I have taken part in them (as a bridesmaid when I was a child) for larger, more formal legally binding wed-dings. It is entirely up to you whether you want to rehearse proceedings or not. I would say that even if you do have a rehearsal, this does not mean things will not go wrong! However, if you are nervous about the handfasting, and most people are to some extent, it may set your mind at rest, even if it means a slight lack of spontaneity.

Should I Hire a Wedding Planner?

You may wish to hire a wedding planner or a wedding coordinator to circum-vent some of these difficulties. A professional can be enlisted to minimize any problems well in advance—and to anticipate any problems that you have not foreseen. Wedding planners and coordinators are usually experienced professionals who have seen it all before and can advise accordingly.

Katrina Otter points out that there is a difference between planners and coordinators:

> *…they're often seen as the same role whereas in actual fact there's a huge dif-ference between the two, which ultimately boils down to the level of service—a planner will usually be for full or partial wedding planning, helping you throughout the planning process from start to finish, sourcing your venue and suppliers, budgeting and RSVP management, and so on. A coordinator, on the other hand, will generally come in toward the end to help you in the final few weeks, pulling together the time line for the day, confirming the suppliers, tying up loose ends, and being there on the day itself.*[31]

---

31. Katrina Otter, "Hiring a Wedding Planner—Who, What, Why, When & Where," January 2017, https://cocoweddingvenues.co.uk.

You may not think that this is necessary, and it will depend on the logistics and circumstances of your handfasting. Most of the people whom I have handfasted have not relied on a wedding planner, because the scale of the handfasting has not really justified one. Also, I have noticed that handfastees tend to be a bit more laid back about the possibility of things going wrong. This may be because pagans tend to be alternative types who perhaps are not quite so invested in making an impression and who are not so concerned about having a day that is perfect in every respect.

Wedding planners UKAWP[32] say that there are a number of reasons why couples hire a planner:

- Limited time
- Location
- Logistics and knowledge
- Coordination
- Planning a large and/or complicated wedding

Wedding planners come from a wide variety of backgrounds—the planner quoted above points out that some come from corporate events management, while others have a stage or costume background, to name but a few. The planner you choose should be someone with whom you feel comfortable and who understands your own particular needs—rather like choosing a celebrant. Check their experience and qualifications, if necessary.

A wedding planner is there to take the burden of organization away from you, but be conscious that you will need to spend a considerable amount of time with the planner. You will need to go through their quote to see how much time you will actually have with them before, during, and after the ceremony. You can book planners for partial or full planning, perhaps if you just want help with, for instance, the reception.

Some venues have a wedding planner attached: note that if you choose this option, the planner will not be independent of the venue, and thus any

---

32. Bernadette Chapman, "UK Alliance of Wedding Planners," https://www.ukawp
    .com.

problems that arise may not be dealt with objectively. You may also find that the in-house planner has their hands somewhat tied. The venue planner may also not be present on the actual day.

Don't be afraid to ask about outcomes. Question them about trouble-shooting: they should be able to answer queries about what action they will take if something goes wrong. Ask them specifically if they have handfasting experience in addition to mainstream weddings. Many professional wedding planners are used to coordinating multicultural events that may take place over several days, for instance.

And for your part, make sure you contact a planner or coordinator ahead of time. Don't leave everything to the last minute. A year in advance is usually a good time frame in which to work.

Tips for the Celebrant 1: "Interesting" Couples

If, as a celebrant, you have strong objections to any ideology expressed by your handfasting couple, there are two approaches you can take:

- Adopt the view that they are entitled to their own opinions and you are there simply to do a job. Registrars, after all, do not usually engage with the political beliefs of their clients.

- Take the view that you should not be asked to participate in a ceremony in which beliefs that are directly contrary to your own would compromise your own integrity.

Both positions are valid: it is a question of your personal mileage. There was a case in the international press in recent years regarding an American Heathen couple who held strong views on the subject of people of different races handfasting one another, and as far as I remember, they had equally strong views on LGBT handfasting. They requested a celebrant who had not handfasted racially mixed couples or gay couples. The Irish celebrant community responded strongly to this and stated that the couple would not be welcome to be handfasted in Ireland.

Celebrants are entirely within their rights to refuse to handfast someone in these kinds of circumstances. This is your choice: do not allow pressure or emotional blackmail (such as accusations of "censorship") to be applied. You can explain to the handfastees that you are not comfortable with their ethical stance and, therefore, you are simply not the right person to conduct their handfasting, as an unpleasant atmosphere at such a ceremony benefits no one.

However, I personally think that diplomatic skills are a plus. I feel that when I am hired as a celebrant for a handfasting, I am there to do a job, not to engage in political debate: we may be representatives of a spiritual path, but our advocacy is limited by context.

I spoke to an experienced celebrant who wishes to remain anonymous, but who has run into a number of issues around handfastings. They say that the main problems include

> the couples who start communicating with us by telling us about their "pagan credentials." If they are Very Important Pagans, they are usually going to be difficult (the worst are the "Wicca Mafia"). This especially applies to any High Priest or Priestess who just won't relinquish control of the magic ... it really is too much to run the ritual and be the people getting married. Just lose the control for one day, please! Strangely enough, these are often the couples who don't get "nice" weather ...
>
> There are also the couples who want, or try, or just go ahead and do, something dangerous. This can range from wearing six-inch heels in mud (we pulled her out and up), to jumping over the broomstick by a cliff's edge (we nearly fainted), to requests for huge fires at scheduled monuments ... and to bungee jumpers. We usually persuade folk out of this or suggest it is more appropriate for the reception. And we've got better at recognizing when a couple have "ambitious plans" and getting in first with a moderate suggestion.
>
> Couples forget to bring rings, cords, relatives, readings, flowers, and paperwork. We get them to give us as much as possible before the ceremony so we know the objects will be present. We remind them to tell guests the time and place. Guests sometimes only arrive as we are finishing. In general, people don't think details anymore, and they don't seem to anticipate problems.

All the above obviously constitutes a tricky situation, and in the end you, as a celebrant, must be guided by your own principles and your own conscience. There is little point in holding a ceremony for someone if you are mutually uncomfortable: celebrants and handfastees need to be a good fit. As a celebrant, do not be afraid to gently turn a couple down, and as a handfastee, do not be afraid to shop around until you find a celebrant who is right for you. Paganism, like it or not, contains a wide range of political and ethical views beneath its broad umbrella, and it should be possible to find a celebrant who is a good fit.

Helen Woodsford-Dean also warns celebrants about being firm with couples who are a little bit less than scrupulous with their celebrants. As a celebrant, be clear about what your role will be and how much you intend to be paid for it.

> *No money, allegedly, but then they invite us to the reception on which they have spent thousands—"but could we just have a blessing for the food and the cake and and and …"*

As a handfastee, be clear with your guests as to what you are prepared to do and not to do. Carys Fisher is a Suffolk-based singer-songwriter who herself had a handfasting some years ago. She told me,

> *The day before, my now-ex's family realized they had transport problems and asked if I could possibly hire them a minibus and driver to bring them the one hundred twenty miles to the venue! I'm afraid I told them I had other things to organize, but thankfully they were able to make arrangements and attend after all.*

And it's important to know yourself, too, and whether you have any specific triggers you might need to work around. Carys relates,

> *I have Asperger's syndrome, and the night before I got completely fixated on the tables for the reception being in the right place and the right order. They were literally all identical tables, but I insisted that they each had to be in a specific place in the room. That was my bridezilla moment!*

Vicar Paul Cudby adds,

Sometimes there seems to be a lack of appreciation of, or expectation for, the mystical. Sadly this is more likely to be on the part of the man than the woman. With time, the less-sure partner may come to appreciate that something did indeed take place because they see it in themselves. There are also occasions when it seems to be all about the event itself without a recognition that this is just the first stage in a lifelong process of deepening commitment.

As celebrant and handfastee, treat all these issues seriously. It's better to think about them up front than to confront them on the day.

Tips for the Celebrant 2: Underage Couples

If you are asked to handfast someone whom you think may not legally be of age, I think it is your duty as the celebrant to check. Basically, you don't want to be roped into a statutory rape charge because some lovelorn fourteen-year-olds, who just happen to look eighteen, have asked you to handfast them.

Teenagers can be headstrong, impetuous, romantic, and defiant: this is part of being a teenager. It is legal in a lot of nations to be married at a young age, so one might question why you shouldn't handfast teenagers. Again, this is a point at which you really need to examine your own conscience. It's a great idea to speak to the parents and find out if they approve, but young people may be seeking a handfasting because there's a family problem and they're looking for alternatives. They may not even be speaking to their parents. The whole area is a minefield, and it's best to ask some hard questions up front rather than find yourself answering some even harder questions later.

Tips for the Celebrant 3:
Handfasting Couples Who Have Other Commitments

Tangentially, this brings up the issue of marriage counseling. I have been approached by couples who are already married to other people and have asked me to handfast them. There can be a number of reasons for this:

- They are separated from their partner and seeking divorce but want to show commitment to their new partner.
- They are separated but their partner refuses to give them a divorce (I've come across this once or twice with people who are married to Catholics).
- They are cheating on their spouse but want to demonstrate a commitment to the person with whom they are having an affair.

Again, this is a case of conscience! Some celebrants will balk at the last one; some will take the attitude that everyone is an adult and it is none of their business what lies in someone else's heart. Should you try to engage in marriage counseling? I would advise against this unless you are actually a qualified marriage counselor or are prepared to work with another celebrant who is thus qualified. Counseling qualifications can doubtless be helpful in this kind of situation. I do not personally have such qualifications and tend to rely on my own judgment and common sense, but these can let you down.

A Word about Handparting

Sadly, sometimes things just don't work out. This is in part why there's such an emphasis in the practice of contemporary handfasting on "a year and a day." If the relationship doesn't last, then the couple are free to go their separate ways. But sometimes one or both handfastees feel that it's right to make a formal separation, and in that case, they may wish to undertake a ritual of handparting. A handparting is akin to a divorce.

In his book on handfastings, Raven Kaldera[33] includes a section on some rituals of handparting, and this may be helpful. Otherwise, I would suggest a framework similar to the ones outlined earlier, which includes drawing a circle and calling the quarters. In the main body of the ritual, one or both partners may wish to express their desire before the gods that they are to be considered as separate, and that any bonds that still tie them should be untied. This can either be done as a visualization on the astral plane or by

---

33. Kaldera and Schwartzstein, *Inviting Hera's Blessing*.

literally cutting the handfasting cord with a knife or other sharp object and destroying it.

Kaldera says, rightly, that both partners should ideally be present, but this may not be possible. He also believes that the absent partner should be informed where possible, although in cases where abuse has taken place, the time and location of the handparting should obviously not be revealed; anything that could result in danger to the abused partner is to be avoided. I do not necessarily agree that you need to inform the absent partner. You may, for instance, not wish to contact them at all for any reason, and this is to be respected by your celebrant. As long as the gods know, that should be enough.

Conclusion

You might be feeling a little dismayed by the time you get to the end of this chapter. You hadn't known that so much could go awry! However, this chapter is here to allow you to anticipate any potential problems in advance so that you don't run into them on the day. Your celebrant will help you with a number of these issues. Forewarned is forearmed. Serious problems can be ironed out in good time, and in practice, the hiccups that will inevitably occur on the day itself are more likely to provide an opportunity for some funny stories later!

Chapter Nine

Let's Get This Party Started!

Don't forget that, after the excitement of the handfasting ritual itself, you then have more of your big day to come. It's a good idea to think about what you want to do once the ritual is over. I often end a handfasting ceremony once the couple have jumped over the broom or completed the proceedings as they wish with a declaration of "Let's get this party started!" It's a signal that the ritual—which we will have closed down by then—is well and truly completed, and it's time for everyone to resume their normal selves again. But you need to put some thought into what kind of reception you want to have. Don't let the energy generated by your ritual dissipate.

In this chapter, we will take a look at the reception itself—at things like food and drink and the all-important venue. We'll consider some of the more mundane logistics as well as some fun aspects of your party!

Planning Your Reception

Remember, the reception is an important part of your day. I spoke to Thelemic practitioner Annabelle, who is based in Glastonbury. She had a handfasting on the Tor to her partner, Sol, some years ago, and she also works as a celebrant herself. She cautions,

We would have planned a more structured schedule for after the ceremony, as it can be like herding cats … and the picnic we suggested didn't really happen. We lost some of the guests, and some people went a bit too wild.

As with every wedding ceremony, what you do afterward is up to you. Many people hire a room at a hotel or pub or have a separate space for drinks if they are holding the ceremony at a wedding venue. This will obviously be dependent on your budget, but sometimes on preference: some people really want to be married from home and to hold the reception there in the heart of the family, too. As with the ceremony itself, it also depends on the time of year. Just as your ritual can be disrupted by rain, an outside buffet can turn from a lovely summery experience into a drenched nightmare unless you have alternative provisions (perhaps in the form of a marquee, for example). And it also depends on your location: Are you holding your handfasting elsewhere in the country? Do you need local knowledge, for example, regarding caterers?

As I've noted in previous chapters, location, both of the handfasting itself and of the reception, is a very important part of your ceremony and needs to be considered with care. This is one area in which you may want to consider the use of a wedding planner, especially if the proceedings are lavish—I know of one handfasting that actually consisted of three separate ceremonies and receptions: one in London, one at Stonehenge at dawn with a wedding breakfast at a nearby hotel, and then a third one elsewhere. In my experience, however, this kind of lavish enterprise is unusual for handfastings, which tend to be on a smaller scale.

In addition, have you looked at the parking situation? A rather mundane issue, but in my experience, problems with parking can make your guests frustrated and irritated more quickly than almost anything else. This is particularly the case with a handfasting with multiple venues that are located far apart, especially rituals that are held in remote areas.

With all venues, the number of guests at the reception will be dependent on the venue's health and safety directives.

Whatever sort of venue you choose, and whether or not you are using a wedding coordinator or planner, make sure you have the contact details of **one main person** at the venue.

Some of the nicest venues I have experienced are farm venues: one was in Somerset with an avenue of flowering chestnut trees, up which the wedding party was carried on the back of a hay wagon, and I also did a handfasting at another venue in Yorkshire where the ceremony was accompanied by a flock of curlews. At this sort of venue, the party or dinner or buffet afterward is often held in a long barn.

These outdoor venues are ideal for after the wedding ceremony. They have a lot of outdoor space, so if you want to hold your handfasting outside, these are ideal. You might even find one that has a purpose-built stone circle, or an area specifically designated for wedding ceremonies. However, they also have indoor space, so if it rains, you can hold the actual ceremony inside and then go to the reception afterward.

Many hotel venues are specifically geared up for weddings, and a lot of hotels make the bulk of their money from weddings, so they are concerned to get it right. These kinds of venues are usually happy to entertain handfastings as well—you can pitch it as a version of a humanist ceremony if you have doubts—and they are usually very professional in their approach. These venues, too, tend to have different locations for the various parts of the ceremony, both indoor and outdoor. One such country house venue near us holds the ceremony itself in a beautiful orangery, while the reception is held in the main house. This gives a sense of progression and structure to the day. The main downside of hotel venues is that they can be expensive and you may not have exclusive use. Are you prepared to field, perhaps, awkward questions about what a handfasting is, or deal with jokes about broomsticks from intrigued but tedious onlookers? Some hotels do offer exclusive-use packages, which are ideal if you want all your guests in one place without the hassle of transporting them to the venue and back.

Marquees can be a lovely venue for a summer reception, but they depend on a number of factors, and you need to give these some thought. A marquee is not, as is sometimes thought, a cheaper option. For instance, is the wedding on your own property, and will you therefore need to contact a marquee company? Will you need a power source such as a generator? Do you have enough bathroom access? Who will be doing the catering? Do you want a single big space or a marquee with a cordoned-off dance floor?

Wedding experts warn that if you are intending to organize a marquee setup yourself, it will take more time than you anticipate, and you will need to go into the logistics with care. This is one area in which wedding experts advise you to hire a wedding planner, because there are a number of considerations involved in organizing a marquee wedding that do not apply to hotel or restaurant-based weddings.

If you have a local pub or restaurant, this can be a great choice for your friends and family. Bear in mind that if your guests are going to include children, some licensed premises may exclude kids from some areas of the building. Are they going to get bored at a sit-down meal and run around? Will you need a microphone for speeches? Will you want to dance at some point? Is there a dance floor—and will a dance floor affect seating? For example, will you need to move chairs and tables around? Experts say that size, floor plan, and sight lines are the biggest challenges you will face with a restaurant reception. The ideal size for these receptions is estimated at around thirty-five to seventy people.

We have done several handfastings in people's homes—for example, in a beautiful house in Essex that had a deck overlooking a boating pond. The weather was dreadful, but this didn't matter as the room itself was enclosed and had French windows overlooking the pond. The reception was held in a conservatory.

Here, your problem is obviously that of space. Unless you actually live in a stately home, most people's houses are not that large, although I have also conducted handfastings in long gardens with buffets (food can be set out in the kitchen and then taken into the garden). The number of guests you will be able to have will be limited, and if they also want to stay with you, there is little respite. Home handfastings are a lovely thing to do, but you do need to work out the logistics, including being watched by the neighbors. Hopefully they know you are pagan, but if not … !

Food for Your Handfasting

What does everyone remember about a wedding? It is often the dress and the food. Most people will recall the food in particular.

I was a celebrant at a disastrous handfasting (which I did not organize, by the way) in which the hog roast had to be collected from a village some miles away. For reasons too complicated to explain, the organizer and I had to go and pick this up in the car, and we couldn't find the place where the hog was being roasted. By the time we came back, the French fries that the wedding venue was contributing had grown cold, and the hog roast wasn't all that warm, either. To put it mildly, the bride was not happy...

Some couples do the food themselves. Sometimes this is really successful, especially if a bride, groom, or both have catering experience or come from families in which large public meals are a common phenomenon. For example, I have a lot of farming relatives who think nothing of supplying several cakes, entire poached salmon, spit-roasted pigs, or sides of beef. However, this doesn't apply to everyone, and my advice for catering is, if you've never done it before, don't think you can do it now. Hire a professional. If you can't afford professional catering, which can be very expensive, then ask around to see if any friends *with the relevant experience* are prepared to do you a very large favor for cost. If you know a venue well, then they may sometimes offer (but don't ask). I am a regular at the central hotel in Glastonbury, a seven-hundred-year-old pub, and the landlady very kindly offered to cater for my father's wake at cost: I ended up spending twenty-five pounds for a buffet for around fifty people. This is great if it happens, but you can't expect it. Similarly, for my mother's ninetieth birthday, a friend made an extraordinary and beautiful cake in the form of a black and a white swan; people are still talking about it some years later. This was a gift for my mother, but again, you cannot count on having generous friends with the relevant experience.

You might also like to take a DIY potluck approach and invite your guests to bring food. Cat Pentaberry in Germany says,

The whole thing had to be affordable. We pared down the guest list A LOT and asked our friends for contributions to the buffet. We had enough on offer for everyone, but it was lovely to have additional delicacies, and this greatly reduced the stress factor for me as my partner doesn't cook and I tend to go a bit overboard when planning to feed my guests at a party.

I would also add as advice to bride and groom: expect about a third of your guests to cancel, but don't count on it. That's why asking people to contribute to a buffet is such a good idea, because the amount of food will correspond somewhat to the number of people who actually show up.

If you decide to have your handfasting professionally catered, it's worth considering in detail what it is you actually want. This will depend on a number of things:

- The location
- The time of day
- The time of year
- The number of guests
- The seating

The Handfasting Breakfast/Supper

If this is a sit-down affair in a local pub, village hall, hotel, or wedding venue, you are going to have to do the math with regard to the seating. Can you fit everyone in? Will it be a tight squeeze? Will there be people who need disability access (such as someone in a wheelchair)? Are there a lot of children among your guests, and are they going to start getting bored or whiny or run about the venue?

If you are holding this outside, where are people going to sit? I personally feel that I have balanced too many paper plates, which wobble, while trying to find somewhere to put a glass, and cutting things one-handed without dropping the plate or spilling everything down my better clothes… If you have a hundred guests and a buffet or a hog roast at which everyone has to queue, how long is that going to take? Are people going to be queuing in the rain, if outside, or in baking heat? If you are inside, is there even room to queue? Are you going to ask people to cut slices of beef with plastic knives? Are some of the dishes likely to slide off the plate? Have you catered for people with allergies or other specific dietary requirements, such as vegetarians and vegans? I have friends who follow Nigerian pagan paths, which have very specific dietary restrictions for religious reasons: Will this apply to any of your guests? If so, is everything clearly labeled?

All these issues are basic, but they can really make or break a handfasting meal and the reception. They are important things to consider if you are intending to do the catering yourself, as happens at a lot of handfastings. If it's a small gathering at a stone circle or hilltop, a picnic is often a viable choice, and I have officiated at handfastings where a cup of coffee out of a thermos and a shop-bought bun have been a perfectly adequate arrangement. As with all elements of your big day, it depends how much trouble you want to go to and how much you are prepared to spend. Also, how far you want to manage your own expectations and those of your guests: you won't get a champagne breakfast on lemonade money. This should go without saying, but expectations around weddings can become unrealistic and get out of hand surprisingly quickly.

Whether your handfasting is held in spring/summer or autumn/winter—and the nature of the weather of those seasons in your region—will affect your catering arrangements. If it's blisteringly hot, you'll need shade at your reception; if chilly and wet, you'll need undercover areas for seating and eating. It's crucial to discuss this in some detail with the venue, and this is one argument for using professional wedding venues to host your reception: they will have organized a lot of ceremonies and hopefully will iron out any problems well in advance.

You will also need to choose your food with care. Winter weddings often benefit from winter food. I attended one where the reception was at a village pub who had simply produced a vegetarian chili and a meat chili with crusty bread, and after a cold morning's ritual outside, this was very welcome. Game stew is another good option, sometimes with added alcohol plus a vegetarian alternative. Roasted vegetables are another good option, and so are baked potatoes. Soup is a good choice for a sit-down meal; wedding sites usually suggest alternative ways of serving this (practical ones—for example, in nice little ornamental cups). I've had a lot of traditional three-course meals at conventional sit-down wedding receptions with waitstaff service, and these work pretty well, too.

For summer receptions, you can go for a lighter touch with salads, fruit puddings, and cold meat and cheese. Buffets work well in summer as long as you have plenty of adequate seating.

Think about whether you want a theme. If you're being handfasted in a particular location, you may want to look up some local specialties. In Somerset, for instance, we have a number of cider farms that produce excellent apple products, including cider itself, but also cheeses. One of our local cider farms provided cider brandy for Prince Harry's wedding. It's a nice touch to use some local produce in your handfasting breakfast/lunch/supper.

The cake is obviously a major part of the proceedings, and some people do go the whole way and make their own if they are keen bakers. I have seen some beautiful homemade wedding cakes. Otherwise, go professional. This can be expensive but is usually worth it, and you don't have to go down the traditional fruitcake route (Meghan Markle's elderflower sponge, for instance, was well-suited to the spring timing of her wedding). Kate and Prince William had a fruit cake, which is a traditional medieval offering: the top tier is traditionally kept for a christening cake. Irish wedding cakes also follow this model, with a top whisky-laden tier also being used for the christening cake. There have been suggestions, however, that the traditional wedding cake was originally a meat or mince pie, and the tiered wedding cake we know so well today was actually inspired by the tiered spire of Saint Bride's church in London. In the late eighteenth century, so the story goes, a local apprentice baker, William Rich, fell in love with a girl, and in order to impress her, he created a magnificent cake inspired by the church spire. Sadly, there is no evidence that this is true, but it is a lovely story, and the spire does indeed look like a big, tiered cake.

The ancient Romans made their wedding cakes from wheat and they were broken over the bride's head. You probably won't want to reenact this particular custom—although it would certainly be memorable!

You may want to link your handfasting to one of the Wheel of Eight festivals: Is there something traditional for the time of year, such as a plaited loaf at Lammas, for instance, or woodruff and strawberry wine at Beltane?

You might also want to take a look at some traditional wedding food around the world:

Bem casados ("happily married") is a traditional wedding cookie from Brazil. Here, two little sponge cakes with a filling of dulce de leche (caramel sauce), egg curd, or jam are individually wrapped, tied with a bow, and presented to guests.

Tang yuan (sweet rice ball soup) is served at Chinese weddings. The smooth little balls must be swallowed whole in order to achieve a smooth and happy marriage. They may also serve **yi mein** (long-life noodles), which are egg noodles with mushrooms and chives and whole fish (the word for "fish" is similar to the word for "abundance"). Similarly, in Japan, **sea bream** is often served at weddings because the word for this type of fish is close to the word for "auspicious" or "fortunate."

In Nigeria, a **kola nut** is shared between the couple, symbolizing the ability of the couple to heal their differences.

Foy thong (golden silk threads) are a traditional noodle dish served in Thailand at weddings. These are strip noodles, as long as possible, put through a cone and made of egg yolks and sugar.

Janchi-guksu (celebration noodles) are served at Korean weddings and have an elemental representation for wood, fire, earth, metal, and water. These may be made of green zucchini for wood, carrot for fire, egg yolks for earth, egg whites for metal, and black seaweed for water.

The Japanese may serve **kazunoko** (herring roe) for fertility and prosperity.

Jordan (sugared almonds) are served at Greek and other Mediterranean weddings, the bitter almond symbolizing the lows of marriage and the sugar coating representing the highs. In Italian, they are known as **confetti**—this is where we get the word for the little pieces of colored paper from.

Hindu weddings may contain an "offering" (*madhupak*) of **honey and yogurt:** honey stands for sweetness and yogurt for good health.

In Bulgaria, **butter-bread** is baked by the bride and her family, and the loaf is torn apart by the couple—rather like a wishbone! Russians, Ukrainians, and Polish families bake breads called **korovai** covered in flowers and sheaves of wheat made out of dough. The korovai is surrounded by a circlet of periwinkles, symbolizing purity and love. Some of these have birds, animals, suns, and moons on them, also made from dough, and can be very beautiful. You might want to look into making a pagan equivalent, particularly when it comes to the "cakes and ale" part of the ritual, if you are intending to include this. Why not have a wedding bread instead? Although you may or may not want to follow the Cretan custom in which the bride throws the loaf in the air. Rather like the bouquet thrown by British brides, the woman who catches the loaf will traditionally be the next to be married!

And finally, one of the most ornate customs is the Persian **ceremony spread** (*sofreh aghd*). This is set out on the table at which the couple say their vows, and in addition to the food, the table holds a mirror to represent the couple's vision of themselves as they go forward into their new life. It also contains a needle and thread (to symbolize the couple stitching together their lives and families), coins for prosperity and abundance, candles, rose water, and either the relevant holy book depending on the religion of the couple or the *Hafez* (a book of classic Persian poetry). Food includes bread, cheese, eggs, greens, walnuts, apples and pomegranates, and a number of spices and incense: poppy seeds, salt, wild rice, black tea, angelica, nigella seeds, and frankincense.

All these foods are symbolic, and you may like to look into your own pagan or spiritual tradition to see which elements might be included in your own wedding feast. There are a number of pagan cookbooks available that have recipe ideas for specific times of the year. Here are a few suggestions:

Beltane: May Wine is often drunk at this time of year, and you can use a bottle of strawberry wine, rosé, or simply a good white wine with a sprig of sweet woodruff—magically associated with sexuality and protection—suspended in it. Strawberries and dishes containing honey also feature at Beltane celebrations.

Summer Solstice: Some pagans bake a round loaf at the solstice, symbolizing the sun, and fruit such as oranges, peaches, or nectarines can be used.

Traditional Midsummer food in Scandinavia includes salmon and herring plus milk and cheese. Honey cookies are an option, too.

Lughnasadh: Baking again features here, since this is a harvest festival, and I've seen celebrations with beautiful plaited loaves. Corn on the cob is a favorite choice, too. Decorate your table with bunches of scarlet rowan berries and sheaves of corn.

Autumn Equinox: This, too, is often treated as a harvest festival. You can include apples and other seasonal fruit at your autumn handfasting reception. The Harvest Moon, the full moon that occurs at this time of year, is also known as the Wine Moon—celebrate this in the obvious way! Check out recipes online for a Mabon Cake, too.

Samhain: Pumpkin pie or soup is a no-brainer at this time of year, and you might consider spicy cookies as well.

Winter Solstice: Some of the traditional seasonal foods at this time of year work well for handfasting food as well, such as a chocolate Yule log, nuts, figs and dates, and baked ham. Cakes celebrating the old witch La Befana, who delivers presents to Italian children around Twelfth Night, can also be made for a handfasting in early January.

Imbolc: Dairy products are associated with this winter festival, and a Bride's Bannock (an unleavened oatcake dedicated to the Goddess Bride) might be something you'd like to try. In Irish lore, if you serve butter on February 1, you have to churn it on the same day (might be a bit much on top of your handfasting ceremony!). Pancakes are traditional for this time of year, too—bringing Pancake Day forward a bit. Rosemary is sacred to this time of year and can be used in food or as table decorations. Some authors also recommend various kinds of milk punch.

Spring Equinox: Add rosemary and lemon balm to wine and serve with grapes to celebrate the spring equinox at your handfasting. Egg dishes (such as deviled eggs) are a good way to mark the festival of Ostara, too.

Some pagans like to "paganize" their hot cross buns, perhaps with a spiral on top or a pentagram.

Whatever the time of year, it might be a good plan to have some symbolic food but also some practical alternatives that can feed large quantities of people—particularly if you are intending to do the catering yourself. You might consider Italian antipasto platters, seafood platters, ploughman's boards, seasonal appetizers, roasted vegetables, pulled pork or a hog roast, or perhaps a vintage afternoon tea.

Drinks

Whether or not you have a bar at the venue is up to you, but it's a good idea to have a combination of alcoholic plus nonalcoholic drinks for the drivers and nondrinkers. For a lot of pagans, mead is a popular choice, and it's an increasingly selected drink among mainstream folk, too: there are more outlets for purchasing this honey-based beverage than there used to be.

Hot drinks are a good option for winter handfastings (as with soup, if you are coming in from a cold and possibly damp ritual, a hot drink is a good idea). Try cocoa with a choice of toppings, such as whipped cream and sprinkles or grated cinnamon, chocolate chips, coconut chips, marshmallows, candy canes, peppermint sticks, or salted caramel sauce. Chai is a good choice, too, and there is a huge range of herbal teas and various kinds of coffee available.

For summer, making your own lemonade is easy, and you can add lime, sprigs of mint and/or verbena, cucumber, nasturtium petals, or lavender.

There are some traditional wedding drinks, too: the Dutch make *bruid-stranen* ("bride's tears"), a mulled wine flecked with gold and silver leaf symbolizing the tears of the bride (hopefully happy ones).

Sharing a drink or a cup is part of many wedding traditions, including pagan ones. Often in other rituals, a cup is passed around the circle of participants from which they sip. In handfastings, couples often sip from the same cup—of mead, wine or fruit juice, or holy water. You don't have to have an alcoholic substance—couples in Java sip sweet tea from the same cup, or a yogurt drink in Bangladesh. The French do use wine in a *coupe de mariage* (marriage cup). *Sabrage*—slicing off the top of your wedding champagne bottle with a sword—might be a bit beyond you unless you are reenactors (it's popular in military weddings).

In the American South, couples bury a bottle of bourbon upside down in order to ensure a dry day: *bury a bottle a month to the day in order to keep the rain away.*

Conclusion

Your handfasting party is an ideal chance for you to show your guests a good time—and to have a good time yourself! You can take this chance to weave pagan elements into your handfasting by including seasonal food and drink. The good thing about handfastings is that they give you the chance to be creative and individual, and this extends to your reception, too.

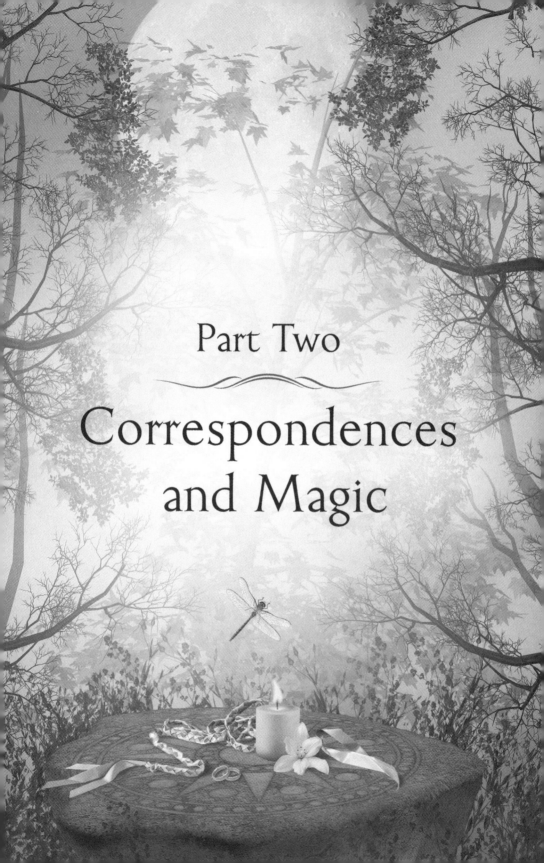

Part Two

Correspondences
and Magic

Chapter Ten

Magic for Unity

Out of all the magic that has ever been practiced in the world, in every country and every time, I would estimate that a large percentage of it has been done in the name of love. This is one of the central aspects of human existence, and this is reflected in the importance given to love by magical practitioners through the ages. Love spells have an ancient history.

In this chapter, we're going to take a look at the history of love magic and how you might incorporate the craft of love into your own handfasting and, subsequently, your marriage. For magic can be done not only to draw love, but to sustain it. We will look not only at some love spells, therefore, but also at rituals for marriage—and some sex magic, too.

A Short History of Love Magic

If we look at the history of magical practice over the last few hundred years in Great Britain, we can basically split it into two kinds: magic done to improve spiritual development, and magic that is results-oriented. In the latter category, magic is done for a range of different reasons, which will be familiar to all of us: getting money (including hunting for treasure), healing oneself or other people, finding lost objects, bringing harm upon enemies or using defensive magic against other practitioners, predicting the future, and finding love.

When we look at what we know of the work of cunning folk—the "people's magicians"—of the medieval period onward, we find that the bulk of their work was done for money; magic was a service industry. There was no state healthcare system in those days, no police force, and a limited legal system. People were largely on their own when it came to looking after their health or making money. You might have been too poor to pay for a proper doctor; you may have had few or no qualifications and been unable to find work that gave you anything comparable to a living wage. Magic thus enters the picture when people have no other recourse and thus become desperate.

Since the Victorian period, things have changed, at different times and in different ways across the world—but changed they have. New social laws have brought in welfare programs and—in Britain and many other countries—a national health system that is free at the point of delivery. All countries now possess a police force and a legal system that, though it may still be imperfect, allows citizens an increased amount of redress in terms of justice. The reasons for approaching a cunning person are still present, but they are now dealt with by other, and arguably more effective, means. If your property is stolen, for instance, you now consult the police or put a photo of the missing item on social media, rather than going to see your local witch. If you are sick, you go to a doctor, or to an alternative healer—perhaps the closest we still have in Western nations to the old kind of cunning person.

The outliers, with which existing state systems are still unable to deal, are divination, cursing, and love magic. Predicting the future remains a chancy prospect, no matter how many "futurologists" are hired by governments. The general public still prefers to consult a tarot reader to "know" the future, whether for fun or because they have a pressing need for questions to be answered that rational methods cannot touch. There is still no way that a straying partner can be brought back into the family fold by means of science or law, other than perhaps therapy or relationship counseling. And although "game theory" activists like to pretend that sexual and romantic attraction are based on a form of psychology that can be used to manipulate women, these methods are dubious, to say the least.

Redress for injustice is usually best sought within the law, but every magical practitioner will have experience of being asked to undertake a curse on behalf of someone, often a person whom the law has failed. Whether the practitioner chooses to go down this route is up to them and up to the tradition in which they are working.

And then there's love magic. It is found in all countries and all cultures and throughout the historical past. Like healing and the other perennial targets of spells, love magic has been around since the very early days. The earliest depictions of love magic derive from the ancient Near East, dating to around 2200 BCE. The ancient Greeks differentiated between the magic of *erôs* and the magic of *philia*: the latter is female, depending on notions of friendship and affection, and the former is male, relating more to erotic love. This distinction reflects Greek attitudes toward gender roles and may not apply to our modern world. *Philia* spells are aimed more toward preserving love and beauty than they are toward attracting another, and they also have the secondary aim of making the spell worker feel more in control: this is a common facet of magical practice that we still find today. Spells of *erôs* are designed to increase lust and desire in the love object and were more commonly practiced by men and sex workers.

We need to remember, when we are looking at the Classical world, that different attitudes were taken toward the practice of magic. For the Egyptians, magic seems to have been a normal part of everyday life and religious practice, but for the Greeks, it was separated from religion and was regarded often as rather seedy and shady. So, to engage in love magic of any kind would not have been a respectable pastime.

Roman women also employed *philia* spells in order to control a partner. This should not be judged too harshly, although magical practitioners today take a dim view of magic that is used to alter another person's will without their knowledge or consent. Remember that women in antiquity had little power: women in the Classical world of Greece and Rome were not permitted to vote, and many were confined to the domestic sphere. Thus, if you have little power, you seek it where you can, and in these worlds, power came from men. Gain power over a man, and you gain power, period.

Christopher Faraone of the University of Chicago, an authority on ancient Greek magic, points out that in the Greek tradition, *erôs*-based love spells are analogous to curses and use techniques that we find in cursing (such as poppets), whereas *philia*-based magic uses the techniques that we find in healing, such as potions, amulets, and knotted cords. He says,

> ...this healing magic, which seems to have been the purview of women, evolved...into forms of philia magic focused on healing or preserving a broken relationship. Erotic magic, on the other hand, is based on cursing techniques and often seems to be used by one family to attack another. Most often it seems to be used by a man who's on the outside of a family trying to get a woman out of her father's house or her husband's house by breaking up a relationship.[34]

Wine was used in *philia*, as were herbal preparations made from plants, such as oleander, the root and juice of mandrake, and cyclamen. The very word *potion*, which makes many people think of love potions, comes from the Greek word *poton,* meaning "that which one drinks."

The Greek book of practical magic, known as the *Cyranides*, contains a love potion. (I would be seriously reluctant to trust a lot of ancient Greek magic: for instance, a fertility charm involves strapping peony flowers and dirt from a mule's ear around your lower abdomen. Just don't go there!) The one in the *Cyranides*, according to psychologist Carl Jung, involves the use of a peacock's brain—you're going to have trouble getting hold of this in the first place! But the word *aphrodisiac* itself comes from the name of the Greek goddess Aphrodite, and the idea that certain foods can generate an erotic effect is found among Classical writers: figs, honey, and oysters, for example, are regarded as aphrodisiacs today. Some of this is what we term "sympathetic" magic, based on the theory of correspondences; oysters, for instance, are probably held to be an aphrodisiac because they somewhat resemble female genitalia, and similarly with figs. In addition, edible bulbs, garlic, onions, leeks, lentils, prunes, mushrooms, myrtle extracts, and carrots were used in love potions—some of this, too, may reflect sympathetic magic, as the long bulbous shapes can be reminiscent of a phallus.

---

34. Christopher Faraone, "Ancient Greek Love Magic," *Fathom Archive*, accessed November 3, 2020, http://fathom.lib.uchicago.edu/1/777777122299/.

The Romans believed that steeping orchid leaves would produce an aphrodisiac effect. Satyrion, an orchid used by the Greeks, was added to wine as an aphrodisiac. Its name refers to the satyrs, the lusty goat-man spirits of Greek legend. As a less fragrant alternative, Roman mystery writer Caroline Lawrence was apparently told by a guide in Pompei that *gloios* (Greek) and *strigmentum* (Latin), the mixture of oil and sweat scraped from a gladiator's body, was sold as a love potion. Lawrence chased this up and found a quote by Pliny the Elder in *Natural History*: small amounts of *strigmentum* changed hands "for the equivalent of a half a million dollars."[35]

Maybe if you're going to go Classical, it might be worth rethinking the peacock's brain idea after all? But don't do what a woman in ancient Athens did in 419 BCE and find yourself in court because you've accidentally poisoned your husband when applying a love potion. We have a speech for the prosecution entitled *Against the Stepmother for Poisoning* by Antiphon (Antiphon was the Athenian orator involved in the trial). The case was brought by her stepson, and she was accused of poisoning not only her own husband, but someone else as well. We don't know what the outcome of the trial was, unfortunately, but it may have been part of an argument about an inheritance.

There are records of women undertaking erotic magic in the ancient world, but they seem to have been sex workers or courtesans—not "respectable" women. Perhaps this is an example of women who transgress by using (or stealing?) men's magic? According to Faraone, sex workers had an almost masculine status: they could own their own houses, and they adopted daughters.[36]

Nor were these spells necessarily between men and woman. We have examples of some same-sex spell craft from the Egyptian papyri: there is a spell listed in which a woman, Herais, attempts to draw to her another woman called Serapis. In true syncretic form, she entreats Anubis, the Egyptian jackal-headed

35. Caroline Lawrence, "Love Potion Number IX," accessed November 3, 2020, https://www.wondersandmarvels.com/2012/09/love-potion-number-ix.html.

36. Faraone, "Ancient Greek Love Magic."

god who is also a lord of secrets, and Hermes, the Greek god of communication, to assist her. Another woman, Sophia, seeks to entrap a lady named Gorgona. This last spell is quite fierce in tone:

Burn, set on fire, inflame her soul, heart, liver, spirit, with love for Sophia …[37]

This does not necessarily mean that same-sex relationships were approved: an appeal to a god of secrets suggests that they may not have been, hence the resort to magic—which is often a last resort.

A Word about Love Spells

After all this, it might be a good idea to add a note about love magic. It's going to be a short note, however, because my view of it can be summed up in a single sentence: DON'T DO IT.

If I have spent longer on any form of magic other than rituals or my own practice, it is in counseling people not to undertake love magic. Mostly, people resort to this kind of spell work when they are desperate, when a lover has left them, and when they are trying to get that lover back. This is almost always a bad idea.

When you split up with someone, you are usually not thinking straight, and you are sometimes tempted into unwise courses of action: stalking on social media, texting the person obsessively, and consulting practicing witches on love magic.

I know a number of people—mostly but not exclusively women—who have done magic to get their love object back, and without exception, they have deeply regretted it. This is often because the type of person on whom we become romantically fixated seems to follow the archetype of the "dark triad": the narcissistic, sociopathic, psychopathic type. This isn't surprising, because those kinds of people work very hard to induce others to become

---

37. Alice Barnes-Brown, "Ancient Greek Sex Lives, God on God Action, Erotic Magic and the Language of Love," accessed November 3, 2020, https://www.historyanswers.co.uk/ancient/ancient-greek-sex-lives-god-on-god-action-erotic-magic-the-language-of-love-nsfw/.

enmeshed with them. Then they leave. In their wake, people get drawn to unwise magical action, such as trying to control their ex through a spell.

To sum up, love magic is controlling magic. It's best avoided. Especially if it works and you end up back with your emotionally abusive partner. It might be what you want—but is it what you need?

My partner tells clients to do love spells for themselves: if you love yourself, your self-esteem (not your ego or your insecurity, which are two sides of the same coin) will turn you into the sort of person whom others love as well, in a healthier mundane way that doesn't need magic to bring the love about.

But can you do a general spell for love, without a specific target, and based on the kind of attributes you'd like to have in a lover? This is far less fraught and can work well in addition to asking the gods and spirits to send you someone whom you'll get along with. Because this kind of magic does not have a specific person in mind, it's generally held to be more acceptable—and you could use a poppet, for instance, making a doll on which could be written the attributes you'd like to attract.

Here, it's the same principle of "like with like"—you're forming a poppet as a simulacrum of a general person, inscribed with the qualities you'd like to draw to you from another.

In the same vein, can you do spells for the success of your marriage?

Absolutely. You might like to consider working with one of the deities who are a patron of marriage, such as Hera, Aphrodite, Genetrix, or Frigga. I'll be taking a closer look at some specific deities of love and marriage in the next chapter, and I will give examples of some incenses and oils you can make. You might also want to undertake a ritual to one of these goddesses—perhaps before the handfasting itself, or maybe after and at the start of your honeymoon, or at the end of the honeymoon when your married life together is about to begin. I give some examples of rituals below, beginning with a few suggestions for magic to be conducted before the handfasting ritual.

Leading Up to the Ritual

Some people treat the period leading up to the handfasting itself as a chance to forge a deeper commitment to a god, goddess, or spirit—singular or plural. Ways of working with this approach include the following:

- A commitment ritual, rather like an engagement announcement in which you affirm your commitment to each other and announce your intention to the gods to undertake a handfasting. This is a little bit like the *sponsalia per verba de praesenti* I mention in chapter 1—and you might like to undertake this with the knowledge that it is quite an old custom in its own right.

- Setting up a handfasting altar, which can remain until just after the ceremony (or as long as you like). On this, you can place candles, flowers, statues of your god/goddess, and things that are to be used in the handfasting as and when you make them—if you plan a hand-crafted approach. Many people make their own handfasting cords, and you can keep this on your altar once you've done so, for an extra blessing.

- Working on a series of intentions for your handfasting, which you might like to reaffirm once a day or simply once a week—whenever you make your other devotions.

- Writing prayers that you or your celebrant can recite in the ceremony itself.

Now, here's a series of rituals you may like to undertake, either before the handfasting as suggested above, or after the ritual, before you embark on your honeymoon, or during the honeymoon itself. I will begin by giving a general list of the things you will need.

Preparation for All Ritual/Spell Work

Ritual and spell work, like cooking, are a lot more effective and relaxed if you do your prep first! Make sure you have everything you need before you draw your circle.

Incense: This can be of the joss stick or loose incense variety. I have given some recipes for loose incense elsewhere, and you may like to make your own specifically created for a particular deity.

Charcoal: If you are using loose incense, you will need to burn it on a charcoal block. You can buy these in packs from local esoteric shops, but you will also find plenty of choices online. They can be difficult to light, so I suggest using a cigarette or oven lighter rather than matches and holding the block in a small pair of tongs so that you don't burn your fingers. The block should "spark," then gradually turn gray, and it should be placed in an incense burner—ideally, a metal or stone one.

Candles: The size of your candle does not really matter, but if you intend to let the candle burn down at the end of the ritual, it is advisable to use a small to medium-size one. Do not leave burning candles unattended. If your candle drips onto an altar cloth, the tried-and-tested remedy is to remove any large blobs of wax, then place a piece of brown paper over the wax and run a warm iron over it; the wax will transfer to the paper.

Water: You will need a small bowl of this. (Water from a holy place is always preferred, but not critical—as long as it's fresh. You can use rainwater if you can gather it and, at an absolute pinch, water from the tap, but you can also buy bottled spring water.)

You will also need specific items for particular rituals. I'll include details of this later.

Once you have completed your ritual or spell work, cleaning up is as important as preparation. Make sure all candles are extinguished when you are ready to leave the ritual space. (If you are leaving the candle to burn down but want to go out or go to bed, extinguish it, and relight it later on once you're on the premises. It will not negate the ritual or spell, and it is safer than burning the house down!) Similarly, with incense, make sure that all the incense has burned away and that the remaining charcoal—which is likely to be ash at this point—has cooled before you get rid of it. Setting fire to your rubbish bin with hot ash is not recommended!

It is also good practice to make sure your ritual space is clean and tidy, both before and after your working.

Ritual 1: A Ritual to Hera, Venus, and Freya for the Smooth Running of Your Handfasting

This is a ritual for you to undertake before your handfasting to facilitate the smooth running of the ceremony. I have selected Hera, Venus, and Freya, but you might wish to choose other deities of love and marriage instead, depending on the pantheons with which you yourself work.

You will need

- Small or medium-size gold, pale blue, and green candles (for Hera, Freya, and Venus, respectively)
- Images of the three goddesses (you will find plenty of examples on the net or in books of mythology), either as a picture or perhaps a small statue
- A small bowl of water
- Some general altar incense, such as a frankincense mix
- A strawberry (Freya)
- A sprig of mint or a single rose (Venus)
- A peacock's feather (Hera)

[Prepare your ritual space and light the incense. Purify the space with the water. Light the first candle, the green one, to Venus.]

You: Great goddess of love, we honor you! We remember the first days and weeks of the love between myself and [your partner's name] and ask you to honor and bless us as we travel forward into the future of our handfasting.

[Offer the mint or rose to the image of the goddess.]

You: Beautiful Venus, accept this offering for the success of our handfasting, we pray.

[Light the second candle, the pale blue one, to Freya.]

You: Great goddess of love, we honor you! We celebrate the deepening commitment of our love and ask you to honor and bless [your partner's name] and myself as we travel forward into the future of our handfasting.

[Offer the strawberry to the image of the goddess.]

You: Wise Freya, accept this offering for the success of our handfasting, we pray.

[Light the third candle, the golden one, to Hera.]

You: Great goddess of marriage, we honor you! We honor the future of our marriage and ask you to honor and bless [your partner's name] and myself as we travel beyond our handfasting ceremony.

[Offer the peacock feather to the image of the goddess.]

You: Faithful Hera, accept this offering for the success of our handfasting, we pray.

[Take a few minutes to close your eyes and imagine how you want your handfasting to manifest: beautiful weather, happy guests, an intimate emotional connection with your partner—and no problems. Imagine this image being sent out onto the astral as a pattern for your actual handfasting.

Once you have done your visualization and made your offerings, close your circle and leave the candles to burn down safely.]

Ritual 2: A Ritual to Hera

As we will see in the next chapter, Hera is a patron goddess of marriage. You might like to print out this ancient poem below to bring luck upon your marriage and place it upon your altar, along with some golden candles and a sheaf of peacock feathers.

Then, Hera combed her hair with her hands
and wove bright braids with it.
Beautiful, immortal braids, descending from Hera's immortal head…
Hera then dressed herself with an immortal dress.

Athena had woven and polished this dress for her
embellishing it with a lot of embroidery.
Hera attached the dress to her chest with gold pins
and with a belt with a hundred tassels.
Hera put beautiful earrings in her pierced ears,
with three gems that were joined like gooseberries
and their grace was glistening greatly.
Above, the wonderful goddess was covered
with a beautiful, soft scarf, white like the sun.
And beneath her shiny legs she wore beautiful sandals ...[38]

You might like to adopt aspects of this ancient poem in honor of the goddess: perhaps preparing a sacred bath with a lily-scented bath oil (lotus or water lily is sacred to Hera).

Apples are also sacred to the goddess: the first apple tree was said in Greek legend to have been created for Hera's wedding to Zeus by the goddess of Earth, Gaia. If it's a spring handfasting, you could scatter apple blossom petals in your sacred bath or over your bed. The pomegranate is also sacred to Hera, so you could place one by the side of the bed, perhaps cutting it in half to share—but be aware that it is a symbol of fertility!

An ancient preparation ritual dedicated to Hera is known as the "bathing of the maiden." This signifies that the woman has moved on from having the status of a *parthenos* (an unmarried girl), and the prenuptial bath is said to be the initial stage of the marital rites. Later, a statue of Hera herself is bathed. The bathing represents a revival or restoration.

During the Hieros Gamos (sacred games/sacred marriage) in ancient Greece, a young woman would walk with a sacrificial basket, followed by unwed maidens of Argos, who would sing to honor Hera. In part, this was preparation for their own status as brides—as bridesmaids are unmarried friends of the bride today (remember the old saying "three times a bridesmaid, never a bride").

---

38. Homer, *Iliad: Book XIV*, trans. E. V. Rieu (London: Penguin, 1950), 170–186.

The day reserved for the Hieros Gamos is January 18, so you might like to dedicate this day to a ritual to Hera if you are getting handfasted in the year to come.

[Prepare and take your ritual bath. Enter your sacred space where you have placed a golden or yellow candle for Hera and a white candle for her husband, the god Zeus. Make an offering to the god and goddess (for instance, honey or honey cake, pomegranate seeds, or incense—a combination of frankincense and willow bark, since willow is sacred to Hera).]

You: I honor the goddess Hera and the god Zeus on their wedding day.

[Recite the following Homeric hymn to Hera and Zeus.]

You: "I sing of golden-throned Hera whom Rhea bore. Queen of the immortals is she, surpassing all in beauty: she is the sister and the wife of loud-thundering Zeus—the glorious one whom all the blessed throughout high Olympus, reverence and honor even as Zeus who delights in thunder." [39]

[Light your candle to Zeus.]

You: "I will sing of Zeus, chiefest among the gods and greatest, all-seeing, the lord of all, the fulfiller who whispers words of wisdom ... Be gracious, all-seeing Son of Cronos, most excellent and great!" [40]

[Once you have done this, spend some time speaking to Hera in your own words, either silently or out loud. Tell her of your thoughts and your wishes for your marriage, your hopes and fears. Take a little time to see if she replies.

Your partner, if male, may wish to do the same with Zeus.

Once you have done this, present your offering. Take a bite of honey cake or a sip of wine, and leave the rest on the altar for the deities. Thank both

---

39. Hugh G. Evelyn-White, *The Homeric Hymns and Homerica* (London, William Heinemann, 1914), Hymn 12 to Hera.

40. Evelyn-White, *The Homeric Hymns and Homerica*, Hymn 23.

Hera and Zeus, wish them well upon their own wedding day, and leave the candles to burn (safely) down.]

A Ritual 3: Ritual to Venus

You can undertake a variety of rituals to Venus, but this is one option. It relies on the concept of correspondences, and it also uses some ancient prayers to the goddess.

You will need

- A green candle (green is the color of Venus, and if you wish, you can take six candles, since this is the planetary number of Venus in contemporary astrology)
- A penny or a small piece of copper
- The symbol of the planet inscribed on a piece of paper (or embroidery, if you really want to make an effort—you can use a green pen to inscribe this symbol or any prayers)
- Green stones (emerald, jade, malachite, or others) or rose quartz (a crystal symbol of love)
- A mirror
- Some incense for Venus (see recipes in the next chapter)
- A sprig of myrtle and some roses ("Give your mistress pleasing mint and her own myrtle and wicker baskets covered in roses"[41])

If you prefer to work at a deeper level with planetary magic and are accustomed to doing so, you may also wish to use the planetary square of Venus and Agrippa's seals. In addition, you may want to undertake your ritual at the correct planetary hour on a Friday (you can look all this up on the net or in an astrological ephemeris). Place all these things on your altar and light the candles.

You might also like to undertake this ritual to honor Venus the Heart Changer on the date of her festival in ancient Rome (marking the foundation of the temple to Venus Verticordia—Venus the Heart Changer), the Venera-

---

41. Ovid, *Fasti: Book IV*, ed. Elaine Fantham (Cambridge: Cambidge University Press, 1998), 865–872.

lia, on April 1—it's not just April Fools' Day! On this day, Ovid says (I have slightly adapted this),

Yours are the Goddess's rites, Latin mothers and brides, you, too, without the headband and long gown…Remove the jewels: bathe the Goddess whole. Dry her neck and return the golden necklace to it; then dress her with flowers and new roses. She tells you, too, to bathe beneath the green myrtle…Appease her with supplicant words. Her power secures beauty and character and noble fame. Venus henceforth named "Heart Changer." Protect, Goddess, your many daughters.[42]

You may wish to read this passage aloud once you have lit your candles, then make your prayers to the goddess. Prayers in Roman times have been described as being a little bit like a letter: you will need to tell the goddess who you are and why you are addressing her. You can say something like this:

Great goddess Venus, I, [your name], come as a supplicant to you with my prayers. I pray for the love that has come to me to stay with me and [your partner]. May you watch over us and guide us through the course of our married life. May the love that you so generously bestowed upon us remain with us throughout all our days, ever deepening and changing, from the first flush of love and passion, to the deep commitment of later life. Bless us, I pray, and ever bestow the sweetness of love upon us.

The items on your altar, such as the penny and the crystals, can be left as permanent offerings to the goddess. If you need to remove them, wash them in running water and put them safely away. Let the candles burn safely down and leave the flowers and any herbs until they begin to wilt, at which point, remove them.

Ritual 4: Hymn and Invocation of Aphrodite

This hymn was originally written by the ancient Greek author Apollonius Sophistes. In the original, it is very long, and so I abridge it here to a couple

---

42. Ovid, *Fasti*, Book IV, 133–162.

of pages. As with the rite to Venus, make sure that the relevant correspondences—crystals, flowers, etc.—are placed upon your altar and that you have some green, white, or pink candles. Light the first candle, a white one, and read this:

Far-shining Aphrodite, hear our prayer!
Thou Laughter-loving Lady, Paphian,
Well-girded, Golden, Sea-born, Cyprian,
Companion, Tender-hearted, or howe'er
It pleaseth Thee to be addressed, attend,
We ask, our words of praise, and send
Thy Grace, because Thou art the source of all
That's charming, graceful, all that doth enthrall
In word or deed, in action, figure, face.

Then light a second candle, a green one, and recite:

Hear! If ever I've appeased Thee,
Now attend my prayer beseeching,
See my hands toward Thee reaching,
Know my love is everlasting!
Lady, grant the gift I'm asking
And appear before us, whether
Now sojourning deep in Nether
Regions with the Queen of Hades,
Or in Heaven with Thy Ladies,
Founts of all allure, the Graces,
Fair Their form and fair Their faces!
I request Thee, leave Thy station!
Grant to us a visitation!
Show to us Thy face delightful!
Let us worship Thee as rightful,
Shapely form that's Thine adoring!

Then light the final candle, a pink one, and recite:

Hear our voices now upsoaring
To the Heavens from our chorus!
Please, we ask Thee, stand before us!
Queen of Twilight, Queen of Morning!
Thou in starry splendor shining,
Aphrodite, hear us calling!
Show to us Thy Form enthralling!
Golden Goddess, we beseech Thee,

Stretch our arms, and long to reach Thee!
Shining Star of Heaven, hear us!
We implore Thee, come Thou near us!
Hear our holy hymn rejoicing

And Thy praises loudly voicing!
Shining Star of Heaven, hear us!
We beseech Thee, come Thou near us!
See our faces toward Thee turning!
Feel the flames within us burning!
Shining Star of Heaven, hear us!
We beseech Thee, come Thou near us!
Show Thy features! Hold us Spellbound!
Come Thou Lady, Goddess, Gold-crowned,
Merciful and Mighty,
Laughter-loving Aphrodite!
A shining star! It's streaking through the skies,
Descending earthward, dazzling to my eyes.[43]

Once all your candles have been lit, sit down in a comfortable place and close your eyes. Undertake a visualization dedicated to Aphrodite: a visit to the goddess's temple. This is based on the middle part of the hymn.

43. Apollonius Sophistes, "Homeric Hymn to Aphrodite," trans. Gregory Nagy, accessed November 3, 2020, https://uh.edu/~cldue/texts/aphrodite.html.

Imagine you are standing on a seashore. It is early morning, and as the sun rises and the sea mist lifts to herald a beautiful day, you see a small white temple standing on the shore not far away. This is the temple of Aphrodite. It is made of glistening marble and is reflected in the calm pools of the seashore. A short distance away, higher on a nearby cliff, you can see a grove of trees: this is the sacred grove of the goddess.

As you look at the temple, you can see a group of women, of all ages, beckoning to you. These are the priestesses of the goddess. You go toward the temple, and they greet you. You climb the steps and are given a garland of mint, myrtle, and roses to wear. When you turn back to the sea, you notice that there is a green light, far out beneath the water. It looks like a candle flame burning behind an emerald. Briefly, the sea churns, and a figure rises out of the foam, a beautiful woman standing on a huge cockleshell. She wears a pale green gown, like seafoam. She glides in toward the shore, standing calmly on the shell with her feet braced and her hands clasped before her. As the shell touches the shore, the goddess steps lightly onto the sand and smiles at you. Her eyes are bright and piercing. You see that she is incandescently beautiful, but in a way that you find hard to describe. But you can feel her power—there is nothing coy about Aphrodite.

"Come," she says to you, with kindness. "Tell me what you seek."

At this point, you will have a few minutes with the goddess, who draws you away from the group of women so that you can speak with her privately. Tell her what is in your heart, what you desire from your marriage, what your heart's desire might be. The goddess listens gravely, and then she smiles again.

"I shall grant you what you wish," she says. "But I do have some advice..."
And then she tells you what it is.

You thank Aphrodite from the bottom of your heart and bow to her. As you straighten up, you see that her lovely form is starting to be encompassed by a glowing, silvery mist, and soon she has vanished away. The priestesses crowd around you, offering their own congratulations for your handfasting, and take you back into the temple, in which you find the portal back to our reality.

The visualization is complete.

When you open your eyes, recite:

Oh Muse! With visions Thou hast filled my soul,
With visions overpowering, for Thou
Hast shown me Golden Aphrodite!

Thank the goddess once more and make sure that your candles are left to burn down safely.

Correspondences for Venus and Aphrodite

Plants: Rose, myrtle, quince, mint, grape (fruit, leaves, and vines), apples, artichokes, laurel, ash, and poplar trees

Gemstones/Metals: Pearl, rose quartz, amethyst, sea glass, gold, aquamarine, jade, sapphire, silver, and copper

Animals: Dove, sparrow, swan, dolphin, bees, and goats

Scents: Rose, stephanotis, musk, verbena, vanilla, incense, and vervain

Colors: Pink, red, white, violet, silver, aqua, pale green (seafoam), and any shade of light blue

You can also offer fire (in the form of candles or a fire in a bowl), flowers, and incense to these goddesses.

Magic for Your Honeymoon

After your handfasting, you might want to give some thought to magic for the honeymoon. If you are thinking that this might be an ideal time to try out some sex magic—you're right! It is.

Opinions on the wisdom of undertaking sex magic vary from those who are strongly opposed to it to those who suggest that, practiced responsibly, it can be a powerful form of magical work. In the context of a committed relationship following your handfasting, this is a great period to give it a try, since ideally you have the time. In this section, I will take a brief look at the history of sex magic, both Eastern and Western, and at some basic exercises.

Obviously, this is something to be taken seriously, even if you have fun doing it! It can be intense, and its results can also be potent, so even if you're experimenting, it is worth doing some research into it first and making sure of your focus. There are a number of good books on sex magic, which I include in the bibliography at the end of this book.

"The rite is a prayer in all cases, and the most powerful [that] earthly beings can employ...it is best for both man and wife to act together for the attainment of the mysterious objects sought."[44]

Aleister Crowley and Sex Magic

Aleister Crowley is often associated in the public mind with sex magic, and his heritage, in groups like the Ordo Templar Orientis, which Crowley founded, still features this type of practice. Crowley appears to have been bisexual, and he undertook magical acts with both sexes; the idea behind this is that sex results in a release of energy that can be harnessed to magical ends.

Crowley was by no means the first magician in the West to engage with this issue. Nineteenth-century occultist Paschal Beverly Randolph wrote about it extensively in his work *Eulis!*, and he is considered an important figure in the history of sex magic by modern occultists. Sex reformer Ida Craddock published a series of pamphlets in the late nineteenth century—*Heavenly Bridegrooms* and *Psychic Wedlock*—which were reviewed by Crowley. Crowley himself claimed that his work *The Book of the Law*, one of his best-known books, "solves the sexual problem completely. Each individual has an absolute right to satisfy his sexual instinct as is physiologically proper for him. The one injunction is to treat all such acts as sacraments. We must use every faculty to further the one object of our existence."[45]

In his work with magical groups, Crowley connected different sexual techniques (for example, masturbation, heterosexual intercourse, and anal

---

44. Paschal Beverly Randolph, *Eulis! The History of Love* (Toledo: Randolph Publishing Co., 1874).

45. Aleister Crowley, *The Confessions of Aleister Crowley* (New York: Penguin, 1979), chapter 87.

intercourse) with different initiatory grades. Some of his work on sex magic was made public, but some was available only to initiates. Most of it is available today, however.

Crowley's relationships with both men and women did not end well. His friend, modernist writer Mary Butts, claimed that his partners had addiction issues, constant pregnancies, and suicide attempts, and she was also critical of the rituals Crowley imposed on his followers.

A central figure of the type of magic founded by Crowley, which he termed Thelema, is the image of Babalon. She is the Scarlet Woman, a goddess based on the woman who rides on the beast in the Book of Revelations. Crowley presented her as a form of Sacred Whore and, to a lesser extent, a fertility figure. He believed that human women could become her avatars on Earth and encouraged his lovers to see themselves as Babalon. But despite this focus on a female figure, Crowley remained firmly in control of the rituals he commanded.

Dion Fortune and Sex Magic

Crowley was not the only British occultist to engage with the question of sex magic. Twentieth-century occultist Dion Fortune also wrote about it in her novels and her nonfiction works. She proposed that a great deal of magical energy stems from the polarity between male and female (nonheterosexual sex is not really addressed in her work). Her 1924 work *The Esoteric Philosophy of Love and Marriage* directly confronts the question of working with sexual energies, and it seems likely that she was influenced by the magical teachings of an earlier group, the Cromlech Temple of the late nineteenth century. Another member of the big Victorian magical society of the Golden Dawn, Moina Mathers, accused Fortune of "betraying" secrets concerned with sex magic, and from new research by James North, it appears that these "secrets" came from the higher grades of the Cromlech Temple.

Fortune was much more concerned with ethics and responsibility than Aleister Crowley. We might question her heteronormativity, but this was not unusual for the time in which she was writing. Her character Morgan Le Fay in *Moon Magic* also uses sexual tension for magical purposes, but Fortune is concerned more with sexual energy in magic than she is with actual sexual practice in magic.

Fortune believed that orgasm "earths" the sexual force, and so does a properly worked magical ceremony. Wiccan symbolism, which was influenced by Fortune's work and by that of Crowley, is based around sex and fertility. Wiccan founder Gerald Gardner conceived of Wicca as a fertility cult. The blade that is dipped into a chalice at the culmination of some Wiccan rites is analogous to the sexual act, and some covens still make sex part of initiation rituals.

Tantric Sex

If you're interested in exploring tantric sexual practices, you need to be aware that these are very different, and a different approach is taken to them in the West as opposed to their Eastern origins. *Tantra* derives from the Sanskrit word *tan*, meaning "to weave" or "to compose," and originally, in the sixth century, took the form of instructional texts supposedly written by a god or goddess and consisting of a dialogue between the two. It is not one single set of practices and is extremely varied: in some of its forms, it relates to the deities of local landscape (springs, forests, mountains, etc.), which need to be appeased by offerings.

Many of these deities are female, and tantra holds that all reality comes from the divine feminine power—from Shakti. This is sometimes a challenging view since the goddesses within this paradigm are not meek and mild, but powerful and often even violent. Some of the female deities of tantra can shape-shift into animals such as jackals. One image from tenth-century Tamil Nadu depicts a goddess wearing earrings made from a dismembered hand and a cobra. These ostensibly alarming images demonstrate the nonsubservient nature of these goddesses: women and the power of the feminine are central to tantric practice.

Not all forms of tantra rely on sexual practices, but a number of early versions of this type of magic rely on the exchange of sexual fluids, particularly semen: male practitioners would have intercourse with the goddesses and demons of the tantric pantheon, personified by yogini (priestesses), in "kaula" rituals. Later practices involved using orgasm to expand individual human consciousness and gain a connection with universal consciousness.

Within tantra, part of the goal is to raise the kundalini, the serpent power of the body, and this can be awakened via sexual means. Tantra became associated with anticolonial politics in India at the start of the twentieth century, but once it was taken up by practitioners in the States, it became what the British Museum tells us was a "cult of ecstasy." It challenged conventional attitudes to sexuality and, along with practices such as yoga, was adopted by the counterculture of the 1960s.

As with other spiritual practices from different parts of the world, tantra and its origins are to be respected. It is an extremely varied set of practices across Southeast Asia, and the observations I will make in this book about cultural appropriation and engaging with other cultures' traditions also apply here. In some Asian forms of tantra, these practices form part of an entire lifestyle, and some may only be carried out if you work with a guru in a teacher-disciple relationship. The forms of tantra you may come across in the West are likely to be less extensive, committed, and intense. Gavin Flood, professor of Hindu Studies and Comparative Religion at Oxford University, tells us:

> It's not all about sex and rock 'n' roll. Tantra is about gaining liberation and power through meditation. It is about flaunting purity rules and using desire to remove desire, a thorn to extract a thorn. It is not the *Kama Sutra*, which posits pleasure as its end. Tantra instead uses desire as one of many tools … Tantra is about threatening traditions to transgress the orthodox.[46]

The Kama Sutra

The *Kama Sutra* is familiar to most people, at least in terms of its title, even if they have never studied a copy. It is the oldest book in the world relating to human sexuality, dating from the second or third century AD and written by

---

46. Gavin Flood, interview with the *Guardian*, September 21, 2020.

the philosopher Vātsyāyana. We do not know very much about this ancient writer, but it is said that he was sent into the Himalayas to persuade the tribes to give up the practice of sacrifice, and that he introduced the legend of the goddess Tara to the hill tribes as a tantric entity. As with other forms of tantra, Vātsyāyana counseled that the practice was to be taken seriously and was not simply about physical gratification. In the *Kama Sutra,* the author writes,

> This work is not to be used merely as an instrument for satisfying our desires. A person acquainted with the true principles of this science, who preserves his Dharma (virtue or religious merit), his Artha (worldly wealth) and his Kama (pleasure or sensual gratification), and who has regard to the customs of the people, is sure to obtain the mastery over his senses. In short, an intelligent and knowing person attending to Dharma and Artha and also to Kama, without becoming the slave of his passions, will obtain success in everything that he may do.[47]

If you're intending to engage in tantric activities, do some research as well as some experimentation and see whether it's for you. If you don't want to go into this quite so deeply, exploring some of the practices in the *Kama Sutra* might also be worth your while. But you might also like to look into practices of Western sex magic and delve into the works of occultists such as Crowley and Fortune. The Great Rite is usually considered to be the main Wiccan piece of sex magic: a ritual that takes the form of a sacred marriage, a Hieros Gamos, in which the goddess enters into sexual congress with her consort, represented or embodied by the High Priestess and her priest.

You can do sex magic for various purposes. It can be goal-directed, using the power of sexual energy to fuel the intention behind the ritual and gain a particular result. Here, sex is used to drive the magic, rather than forming the focus of the ritual. However, you can also undertake sex magic with the intention of sending that energy forward into your new marriage. Practitioners of sex magic suggest that you first create a *telos:* an intention. This could be, for example, "May our passion continue to burn brightly through-

---

47. Lars Martin Fosse, *The Kamasutra* (Woodstock: YogaVidya, 2012).

out our relationship," or, "May the love that we have for one another be sustained throughout our marriage." You might choose an image to accompany your intention, as imagery is very powerful within magical practice. You might, for instance, choose a tarot card such as the Lovers or the Two of Cups and focus upon this, perhaps placing it for a time upon your altar. Choose a tarot deck that you really like. Or you can draw an image on the astral: work together to create an imaginary picture of yourselves (perhaps as two old people holding hands, to symbolize the length of your relationship, or as parents if you wish to have children).

Practitioners of sex magic suggest that you begin by slowing down. Focus on sensuality rather than on your sexual practice. Concentrate on your partner, and slow down if you think you are approaching orgasm. Practitioners recommend slowly building sexual intensity.

Do not worry overmuch about "achievement"; if you do not climax, don't worry about it. However, if you have built up a level of sexual intensity such that climax is approaching, hold the image of your *telos* in mind (this might take practice), and at the point of orgasm, send that image out into the universe, powered by the voltage of sexual energy. Once orgasm is over, let the image of the *telos* drain from your mind: you have sent it into the universe, and it will now do its work.

Conclusion

Love and sex are hugely important to us as human beings, and this is reflected in magical practice throughout the ages, as we have seen in the course of this chapter. From the ancient Greeks, Romans, and Egyptians, to Renaissance Europe and Victorian England and beyond, magic for love and sex has been a feature of esoteric thought. Take it seriously, both before and after your handfasting, but remember that it's also a chance to have fun. If it's an area of magic that you're not familiar with, this is an ideal opportunity to explore it.

Chapter Eleven
Deities of Love and Marriage

There are many gods and goddesses of love and marriage, and they are found throughout the world in all periods of history. Most people know at least one of them—Venus, the beautiful morning and evening star, who while I was writing this book shone brightly in the sky at her closest point to Earth. Hopefully, her light informed some of the thoughts on these pages.

There are many other deities of love and marriage as well. The Classical world had several, and so did the Egyptians. Such deities are found throughout Asia, too, with some poignant stories attached, and the African traditions have a number of goddesses who relate to the various aspects of love and who are invoked in weddings. I think it is safe to say that there are few—perhaps no—parts of the world that do not pay homage to a god or goddess of marriage and love in some form.

Love is a huge part of the life of every culture, as we saw in our previous chapter, and of every religion. In this chapter, we're going to take a look at some of the many gods and goddesses of love and marriage of the world, how to invite them into your handfasting ceremony, and how to work with them.

Some of these deities are specific to marriage and romance, but some have wider attributes as well. You do not have to have been working for a long time with a deity in order to ask them into your handfasting—but I think many pagans would counsel that it is a matter of courtesy to at least introduce yourself beforehand, perhaps by means of a ritual dedicated to the deity in question in the weeks or months before the handfasting itself. After all, you would probably prefer to make contact with, and introduce yourself to, your celebrant, so why not to a presiding deity, too? Some of the rituals mentioned previously, such as the ones to Venus and Hera, might be a suitable way of doing this.

You might be wondering how to work with a deity in your handfasting. There are a number of ways you can do this:

- Ask your celebrant to invite the deity to watch over the handfasting when they call the quarters at the start of the ceremony (and thank them when the circle is once more closed).
- Ask the deity to bless your union once you have said your vows.
- Make your own personal evocation to the deity; people often do this if they have a long relationship with the god or goddess in question.
- Use candles or flowers or other symbols of the deity in the ceremony itself.

You may feel drawn to a particular god or goddess, either from the ancient world or as part of a living tradition such as Vodou or Hinduism, with whom to work in your handfasting. I would note here that it is usually more appropriate to work with deities of other cultures if you have some heritage within that culture. Cultural appropriation is a genuine issue; you do not have automatic rights to the deities of other cultures.

However, it can also be said that there is a belief in some forms of Vodou that everyone on Earth, whatever their nationality or race, has a guardian orisha: an "owner of the head." If you feel a particular connection to Vodou deities such as Oshun and do not come from the cultural background associated with this particular path, it is worth checking this out with an experienced practitioner and finding out how to approach the deity with respect. Similarly, other religions such as Hinduism or Buddhism are often welcoming to genuine seekers.

If we believe that deities are real, then it may well be the case that they approach us—that they want us to work with them. If this is so, the god or goddess will usually let you know—but this does not mean that you are in some way superior or know more than those who have spent a lifetime in a tradition or whose ancestors have followed it for hundreds or even thousands of years. Respect and humility are key qualities here.

Many pagans are keen to invite the deity with whom they work, and to whom they may have dedicated their lives, into the handfasting circle, but it is also possible to work with one of the many gods or goddesses of love and marriage, too, and we shall look at some of these now.

Áine

Áine is an Irish deity and held to be a goddess of love and beauty. She is associated with Midsummer and is a solar power along with her sister Grian. It has been suggested that Áine represents the light half of the year and the summer sun (*an ghrian mhór*), whereas Grian symbolizes the dark half of the year and the winter sun (*an ghrian bheag*). Áine protects animals and crops and is sometimes associated with the fairy kingdom, with suggestions that she herself is a fairy as well as, or instead of, a goddess. Accompanied by a swan or roan mare and crowned with stars, Áine is a romantic figure.

She is a very appropriate deity to invoke at a handfasting celebration, given her reputation as a deity of love and summer, especially if your ceremony is held around Midsummer or Lammas. You might want to dedicate a ritual to her at the closest festival to your ceremony and ask her to preside over your handfasting.

Aphrodite

The goddess of love—but originally, it is likely that she was Phoenician and not really a love goddess at all! She appears to have been an early fertility deity. But like many of the gods, she had different personae:

- Aphrodite Urania: The goddess of pure, ideal love.
- Aphrodite Genetrix / Nymphia: The goddess of marriage.
- Aphrodite Pandemos / Porne: The goddess of lust and prostitutes (the word *pornography* comes from the Greek *pornographo*: "writing about prostitutes").

There was also a cult involving a Bearded Aphrodite. Both Venus and Aphrodite have a mixed-gender aspect, and I will return to this when I look at Venus a little later on.

Paphos in Cyprus and Cythera in Crete were the centers of the worship of Aphrodite. Her statues were often modeled on courtesans and were thus a little bit scandalous. Unlike some other beautiful goddesses, she was not severe or haughty, but sweet and smiling. She had many amorous adventures and relationships, like being married to Hephaestus, the blacksmith god. But although she seems like such a benevolent goddess, she was able to drive people mad with passion—thus causing all the chaos that suddenly falling in love with the wrong people results in!

You might like to choose one of her aspects, such as Aphrodite Genetrix/Nymphia, to preside over your ceremony. Roses, myrtle, and pomegranates are sacred to her, and so are doves and swans, if you are looking for symbols to include in your ceremony.

You might want to celebrate some aspects of the Afrodisia (Αφροδίσια) festival, dedicated to the goddess, in the year of your handfasting. This took place in the ancient world during the month of Hekatombaion: the third week in July to the third week of August. Some pagans who follow the path of Hellenic Polytheistic Reconstructionism celebrate Aphrodisia for three days around the 4th of Hekatombaion in the Attic Calendar (July and August in the Gregorian calendar). Furthermore, the fourth day of each month is sometimes held to be a sacred day for both Aphrodite and her son Eros, whom I'll consider shortly, so you might consider undertaking a ritual on the fourth day of the month in which your handfasting is held.

Astarte

Both Aphrodite and Venus may have their conceptual origins in the ancient goddess Astarte, the Canaanite queen of heaven, goddess of love and war. The goddess Ashtoreth, who is mentioned in the bible, may also be a version of Astarte—her name combined with the Hebrew word for "shame." She has a sister, Anath, who closely resembles her, and they may both be the root of the Aramaic goddess Atargatis. She is also probably related to Ishtar.

One of the great goddesses of the Middle East, worshipped from the Bronze Age and particularly across the Phoenician city-states such as Tyre and Sidon, Astarte inspires and is syncretized with a number of Egyptian and Classical deities. As one of the oldest deities of love, she is an appropriate choice for a handfasting, although, as with Ishtar, you may find that you have to put some work in: she is not a goddess to be taken lightly. In Egypt, she became associated with the lioness-headed goddess Sekhmet, and one of her animals is the lion, along with the horse, sphinx, and dove, but she was also linked to Isis. A star inside a circle—the symbol of the planet Venus—is also one of her connections and, like the later Venus whose depiction she seems to have influenced, Astarte was seen as a personification of the beautiful morning and evening star. The Greeks connected her with Aphrodite, despite her warlike aspects. She is a popular goddess among witches and Wiccans. In Sidon, Astarte shared a temple with Eshmun, the Phoenician god of healing.

If you wish to invite Astarte into your ceremony, a star within a circle—a pentagram, in other words—is an appropriate symbol to use.

Blodeuwedd

In the *Mabinogion*, the old book of Welsh legends, the story of Blodeuwedd (pronounced *Blod-i-weth*) begins when the hero Lleu, the son of the goddess Arianrhod, desires a wife. Arianrhod gives birth to Lleu before the entire court of her father, Math, in an oddly perfunctory way, and then denies him a name and weapons of his own. His uncle Gwydion has to trick her into providing both. Disguised as cobblers, he and Lleu go to Arianrhod to make her a pair of shoes. Lleu throws a stone at a wren and strikes it between the tendon and the bone of its leg. "The bright one has a steady hand!" exclaims Arianrhod, and this remark—"Lleu Llaw Gyffes"—forms the basis of Lleu's new name. Angered, his mother then curses her son with a further "tynged" (curse)—that he will never have a human wife, so Gwydion later creates a wife for Lleu out of flowers: oak, broom, and meadowsweet. This is Blodeuwedd.

Blodeuwedd weds Lleu, but when Lleu is away, she sees a hunter, Goronwy, and falls in love with him. They learn that Lleu can only be killed if he places himself in a very peculiar position—standing with one foot on a cauldron and the other on a goat! Blodeuwedd tricks Lleu into adopting this posture and Goronwy shoots him with an arrow, but instead of dying, Lleu changes into an eagle and flies away. Gwydion goes in search of his transformed nephew and finds him at the top of an oak tree in the Nantlle Valley, decaying and rotting. He restores Lleu back to life and nurses him to health, then transforms the unfaithful Blodeuwedd into an owl. Thus, as a goddess, she has a dual aspect: flowers and owls, the light and the darkness.

If you are inviting her into your handfasting ceremony, it is likely you will want to work with her in her flower aspect: branches of broom, oak, and meadowsweet are her symbols, and appropriate for a summer wedding.

Epona/Rhiannon

Both Epona and Rhiannon are versions of a very early horse deity, perhaps the deity to which the white chalk horses on British hillsides were dedicated. As we see in the story of Pwyll, Rhiannon married this Welsh hero after many tribulations and is the mother of Prince Pryderi. Shortly after his birth, Pryderi goes missing, and Rhiannon is blamed for his murder by her female attendants, who seek to shift the blame onto her to save themselves. Pwyll spares her life but obliges her to sit at the palace gate and tell her story to anyone who comes by. She also has to carry them on her back to the court, like a mare. Eventually it is revealed that a monster captured the baby: the child is found by a man named Teyrnon and adopted. Later, the boy, now seven years old, is returned to Rhiannon, and that's when he gets his name—Pryderi, which means "worry."

However, later in the *Mabinogion*, Pwyll dies, and Rhiannon remarries the sea god Manawydan and goes on to have other adventures. (We may speculate that this is an example of different tribes mingling and merging and "marrying" their stories together.)

Rhiannon can be welcomed with narcissus and daffodils, the Welsh national symbols, if you are having a spring wedding, but otherwise any white flowers are sacred to her. She is an appropriate choice of presiding deity for anyone who works with horses.

Eros and the Erotes

Eros appears in ancient Greek sources under several different guises. In early sources, he is one of the primordial gods, and he is therefore involved in the development of the cosmos itself. He's thus recognized as a powerful entity—which, of course, love really is! He is often regarded as the protector of homosexual love between men; thus, if you are a gay couple, you may wish to involve him in your handfasting.

In later texts, Eros is presented as the son of Aphrodite. He intervenes—often with serious consequences—in the love life of humankind. The satirical poets represent him as a blindfolded child who cannot see the trouble he causes. This child later becomes the Renaissance Cupid depicted in numerous paintings with his bow and arrows. But in early Greek poetry and art, Eros is an adult and an artist, less innocent than blindfolded Cupid.

Pre-Classical Greece had a cult of Eros, but this was not as important as the cult of Aphrodite. In Thespiae, there was a fertility cult devoted to Eros, however, and in Athens he was worshipped along with his mother. The fourth day of every month was sacred to Eros as well as to other deities, such as Aphrodite herself and Hermes, the god of communication.

According to Hesiod (circa 700 BCE), one of the most ancient of all Greek sources, Eros was the fourth god to come into existence, after Chaos, Gaia (the Earth), and Tartarus (the Abyss or the Underworld). Eros is here presented as a primal force, a power that causes change throughout the world. Parmenides (circa 400 BCE), one of the pre-Socratic philosophers, tells us that Eros is the first god to come into existence.

The Orphic and Eleusinian Mysteries featured Eros as an early deity, but they do not suggest that he is primordial, since they believed that he was the child of Night (the goddess Nyx). Since physical love is often practiced at night, this makes a degree of sense. Aristophanes (circa 400 BCE), influenced by Orphic tradition, tells us of the birth of Eros:

> At the beginning there was only Chaos, Night (Nyx), Darkness (Erebus), and the Abyss (Tartarus). Earth, the Air and Heaven had no existence. Firstly, blackwinged Night laid a germless egg in the bosom of

the infinite deeps of Darkness, and from this, after the revolution of long ages, sprang the graceful Love (Eros) with his glittering golden wings, swift as the whirlwinds of the tempest. He mated in the deep Abyss with dark Chaos, winged like himself, and thus hatched forth our race, which was the first to see the light.[48]

In later myths, Eros was the son of Aphrodite and Ares, the god of war, and he is one of the *erotes* (Greek ἔρωτες). He is thus just one of many winged gods who are devoted to love and sex, including:

- Anteros ("love returned"—he avenges unrequited love and is often depicted with butterfly wings)
- Himeros ("impetuous love")
- Hedylogos ("sweet talk")
- Hymeniaos ("bridal hymn")
- Hermaphroditos ("hermaphrodite"—the original male deity becomes merged with the water nymph Salmacis because they cannot bear to be parted)
- Pothos ("longing")

The Greeks tended to divide emotions in quite a sophisticated way, and the *erotes* reflect this. Part of Aphrodite's retinue, these deities are often associated with same-sex marriage, so as with Eros himself, you may want to consider working with them if you're having an LGBT wedding. They are usually winged, usually male (but may be accompanied by maidens), and usually cause a lot of trouble: spells to attract them or deter them are found in ancient Grecian magical practice.

Eros himself was initially connected to athletics: you find statues to him in Greek *gymnasia*. He was often shown carrying a lyre or the bow and arrow with which Cupid is later associated, and he is sometimes accompanied by dolphins, flutes, roosters, roses, and torches.

---

48. Aristophanes, *The Birds*, 414 BC.

He [Eros] smites maids' breasts with unknown heat, and bids the very gods leave heaven and dwell on earth in borrowed forms.[49]

Both Aphrodite and Eros, some of the other *erotes*, and the Roman Venus are good deities on which to call for your handfasting, and you might want to consider creating a wax figure in their honor—rather in the manner of Classical magic instead of a fabric poppet. Use the descriptions above to dedicate the image to one of these love gods and goddesses, and you can use all or any of the symbols of love to put before the image on an altar or little shrine:

- Red roses
- Images of hearts
- White feathers
- Scallop shells (a symbol of Aphrodite)

Erzulie Freda

If you're working within the Vodou tradition, the goddess/lwa to whom you need to address your prayers is Erzulie/Ezili, the Haitian-African spirit of love, luxury, beauty, jewelry, and flowers. She wears three wedding rings for each of her three husbands—Damballa, Ogun, and Agwe—and she has the title of "Metres," or "Mistress," as she is seen as more akin to a mistress than a wife! She is seen as a tall blonde woman and is very beautiful. Mater Dolorosa is her counterpart in the Catholic tradition.

Erzulie's colors are gold, pink, white, and blue, and her symbol is, appropriately, a heart, plus she often carries a mirror and a fan. She is compassionate and sympathetic toward people in love, but she is also seen as lazy and has a more difficult side (rather like Aphrodite, in fact). She is one of a group of spirits who represent different kinds of love—motherly, grandmotherly, protective, and erotic. Erzulie Balianne helps people forget lost loves and keep secrets. Erzulie Yeux Rouge (red eyes), as her frightening name suggests, takes revenge on faithless lovers. This group of spirits covers all the different manifestations of love in their positive and negative forms, and they are helpful if you appeal

---

49. Seneca, *Phaedra*, 54 AD.

to them. They are rather similar to the *erotes*, as they represent different aspects of love.

However, although Erzulie has female followers, she is said not to care for women very much, and she is often considered jealous of them. She prefers men—as her title of "Mistress" suggests. If you are a woman, therefore, you need to think very carefully before you work with her, and if you do, make sure you treat her with great respect and follow any instructions from experienced practitioners with care. Erzulie is frequently called upon to assist with love spells, as this is one of her areas of expertise. If you are a gay man, however, you have an advantage, because she is supposed to be a patron of gay men.

Offerings to Erzulie include the following:

- Lace
- Perfume
- Mirrors
- Sweet orange liquor
- Bananas fried in sugar
- Rice cooked with cinnamon
- White wine

She values cleanliness, so if you are intending to work with her, make sure the designated space is immaculately clean.

As with all orishas—and indeed, most deities—it is advisable to build up a relationship with Erzulie if you wish to work with her. Don't just show up and ask her for something!

Frey/Freyr

An agricultural deity, the Norse god Frey is associated with fertility. He is one of the Vanir, an earlier deity than Odin or Thor. Frey has a number of magical items: he rides a magical boar, and he also has a ship that can be folded into a pouch when it is not being used. He has a sword that flies through the air independently. His sister is the goddess of love, Freya—together, they represent sex and love. His name probably means simply "Lord."

If you are intending to work with him in your handfasting, you may wish to have a sword on the altar and perhaps use it to draw your sacred circle.

Freya

As the goddess of love, Freya is beautiful. She is called upon in childbirth, but she also has strong magical powers. Her name means "Lady" (hence the modern German title "Frau"). She is immortalized in the story of Brisingamen, her magical necklace.

Like other Norse deities, Freya has the power to shape-shift. She owns a feather cloak, which permits her to take the form of a bird and fly about the various realms. She rides in a chariot drawn by cats and is thus seen by many modern pagans as a cat goddess. When brides are married in fine weather, it is said to be a sign that they have "fed the cat well." Like her brother, Frey, she is also linked to a magical boar, Hildisvini ("Battle Swine"), and this is a sign that she is a warrior goddess. If you are interested in the Norse traditions, both Frey and Freya might be appropriate deities with whom to work in relation to your handfasting, and so might Frigga.

Since cats are sacred to Freya, you might like to have a little image of a cat on your handfasting altar or a piece of jewelry or embroidery that features cats.

Frigga

Frigga is the wife of Odin and, like Hera/Juno, a goddess of marriage and childbirth. The birch is sacred to her, so you may like to invoke her to bless your birch handfasting broom. She also has an association with polyamory—though fiercely loyal to Odin, she nonetheless has links with other men, partly, it has been suggested, as a reflection of Norse customs of hospitality. There are indications that some women married groups of brothers, for instance.

Mint, alder, borage, and rose are also sacred to Frigga. Depending on the time of year, you might like to choose some of these plants to decorate your ceremony or use a birch wand on which to place your handfasting rings or to carry the cord.

Hathor

"Thou art the Mistress of Jubilation, the Queen of the Dance, the Mistress of Music, the Queen of the Harp Playing, the Lady of the Choral Dance, the Queen of Wreath Weaving, the Mistress of Inebriety Without End."[50]

Hathor is the gentle cow-headed goddess of love and motherhood. As Mistress of the West, it is she who welcomes the dead into their new life, and she also assists women in childbirth. The Greeks associated her with Aphrodite.

She is sometimes said to be the mother, daughter, and wife of the god Ra, but she is the consort to a number of gods. A very old name for her is Mehturt, meaning "great flood," a reference to the Milky Way and to the rising of the Nile, critical to the success of Egyptian agriculture.

The Middle Kingdom story *The Tale of the Herdsman* features a herdsman who meets a hairy, alarming goddess in a marsh—but he later encounters her as a beautiful woman. This is similar to a number of tales in which goddesses or fairies can take opposite forms. Hathor appears in several poems in which people entreat her to bring their lovers to them.

But she has a dark aspect, too, as it was Hathor whom Ra sent to punish uprising humans, and the aspect Hathor took on was that of the avenging lioness, Sekhmet, who then became a separate entity in her own right.

If you wish to invite Hathor to bless your handfasting ceremony, the sycamore tree is sacred to her. You can also place cow horns on your altar, or simply a glass of milk.

Hera/Juno

Robert Graves suggests that Hera's name comes from the Sanskrit *Svar* (sky). She was originally a sky goddess, just as Zeus was a sky god. Graves suggests that their marriage was the merging of two different cults.

Associated with the peacock, lion, and cow, Hera is the long-suffering wife of Zeus, though she is also his sister. She is commonly described as "cow-

---

50. Hymn to Hathor, "The Faery's Gifts," accessed November 3, 2020, https://murfeelee.tumblr.com/post/157820672285/.

eyed," but she was held to have been extremely beautiful. Her husband's continual affairs are shown as being a source of jealousy and distress to her, and she takes vengeance on the nymphs and humans whom her husband seduces. She was principally worshipped in Argos.

She is a goddess of marriage, childbirth, and motherhood. She has aspects of an earlier "great mother" of animals, as do Demeter and Artemis. She is sometimes shown as holding a pomegranate. But she is also worshipped as a virgin goddess, her virginity renewing itself year by year—maybe this is a sign that the dutiful and constantly betrayed wife Hera had more independence than she appeared to have. And in Stymphalus, three temples were consecrated to her as child, wife, and widow—perhaps a hint of the maiden-mother-crone imagery that Graves is usually considered to have introduced to modern witchcraft.

She also engages in constant trickery in turn: Zeus has a lover, the nymph Io, changed into a cow, and Hera, who is still suspicious, places it under the protection of the hundred-eyed giant Argus, who can continually watch the nymph/cow. Hermes lulls him to sleep and cuts off his head, so Hera takes the eyes and places them in the tail of the peacock to honor him.

Zeus comes to her first in the form of a cuckoo, and she warms the cold little bird at her breast, getting a bit of a shock when he transforms into her brother and seduces her.

Her Roman counterpart, the wife of Jupiter, is Juno. Like many of the deities whom we have considered, Juno also has some different names and roles:

- Juno Pronuba: Arranges marriages
- Juno Moneta: In charge of marital wisdom
- Juno Domiduca: In charge of the threshold of the new home
- Juno Nuxia: Guardian of the lintel and doorways
- Juno Cinxia: Unknots the marital girdle
- Juno Regina: Aids the new wife in her domestic duties

And she has other forms to guide the woman through pregnancy, too.

There is a temple to Hera Lacinia, or Juno Lacinia, in Agrigento, Sicily. There is a custom that local brides still sometimes leave their wedding bouquets there.

You may choose one of her aspects with which to work at your handfasting, since she is so closely associated with marriage. Peacock feathers can be used to symbolize her, along with pomegranates, willow fronds, and water lilies.

Iduna/Iðunn

Goddess of immortality and the spring, the Norse goddess Iduna carries apples with her to confer everlasting life upon people. There's a suggestion here that she is originally a goddess of fertility, one of the deities of growth and the cycles of the living world. She is the wife of the god Bragi.

As a result of one of Loki's tricks, Iduna is kidnapped and deprived of her magical apples, and thus the gods begin to grow old. They force Loki to rescue her from her abductors, which he does by taking the form of a falcon, changing her into a nut, and flying away with her.

If you wish to work with her during your handfasting, make an offering of apples upon your handfasting altar, or apple blossom if you are having a springtime wedding ceremony.

Ishtar

One of the goddesses of the ancient world, the Mesopotamian deity Ishtar/ Inanna is a goddess of love and war, among other things. Worshipped for thousands of years, Ishtar has astronomical associations: she lives with her father, the god of the moon; her mother; and her brother, who is a solar deity. Ishtar herself is connected to Venus in the forms of the morning and the evening star. Her legend is mainly revealed in the *Epic of Gilgamesh* and Ishtar's *Descent to the Netherworld*.

In the first story, Ishtar falls in love with the hero Gilgamesh, who cruelly rejects her (comparing her to a battering ram, which is something no girl wants to hear, quite frankly). Ishtar borrows the Bull of Heaven to go up against Gilgamesh, but the hero and his best friend Enkidu kill the bull, foiling Ishtar's plan.

In the latter epic, Ishtar descends to hell and undergoes various trials. She is often seen as married to Tammuz, a shepherd. She has many associations but is held to be the first known goddess of love in the world and is connected to love and sexuality. She seems to have had divine links to the Mesopotamian kings, taking the role of mother, sister, and lover. She is an embodiment of the divine feminine. Like many ancient goddesses, she is not simply associated with love, but with many other aspects of human existence: sometimes this is because the original deity has become syncretized with other tribal deities as societies merge and come together.

She is a goddess of considerable depth, and it would be a mistake to take her lightly: only undertake ritual work to her if you are prepared to "go deep": Ishtar, after all, travels down to the underworld and is literally dismembered and remade.

Her symbol is the eight-pointed star, and the lily is also sacred to this ancient goddess. Innana's symbol is a bundle of reeds, representing the reed boat the goddess creates during a great flood to save humanity.

IxChel

IxChel (*ee-shell*) is the Mayan moon goddess associated with love, among other things. Her name means "Rainbow Woman," and she is linked to fertility: women would make pilgrimages to her temples to ask for her help. She is often represented with her companion rabbit, and she sends dreams to both weavers and healers, as she is the weaver of the sacred fabric of life.

If you wish to work with this deity in your handfasting, rainbows are her sacred symbol, along with passion flowers and moonstones.

Kamadeva

Kamadeva (Sanskrit: कामदेव) is the Hindu god of love and desire, along with his consort Rati. He is the son of Vishnu and he is portrayed as a handsome young man with a sugarcane bow, the string of which is soaked with honey. His five arrows are symbolized with flowers: white and blue lotus, jasmine, mango tree flowers, and Ashoka tree flowers. These arrows are silent, representing the way love can strike suddenly and without warning. In the West, the god Cupid has a similar function.

He is accompanied by a cuckoo, a parrot, and bees and is sometimes depicted riding an elephant. He is a god of spring, and his associations are related to spring, too. The goddess of spring, Vasanta, often accompanies him, and his main festival, Holi, is held at this time of year.

If you are moved to work with him, the best way to do this is by reciting his mantra for a set period of time. The usual caveats against love magic apply here, as Kamadeva's mantra is sometimes used either to hold someone's affection or to entreat a former lover to return to you. Do remember that Kamadeva is part of the living tradition of Hinduism: unlike many of the ancient deities, his worship is still very much contemporary, and this should be respected by those from other traditions.

Oshun

Oshun is a Yoruba orisha, or deity. She is a creative force and a nurturing one: the spirit of fertility and love. Associated with rivers, which often fertilize and maintain the land around them, we can see why Oshun has the powers she does. She is the only female orisha of the original seventeen deities sent to Earth, and the youngest, created when the great creator, Olodumare, realized that the world was lacking sweetness. Beautiful, sensual, and powerful, she is sometimes seen as the wife of the thunder god, Shango.

The Nigerian city of Osogbo holds a festival in her honor every year on the banks of the Oshun River, and there is a nearby forest shrine to the orisha, now a designated UNESCO heritage site. She has also been adopted by the African diaspora in places such as Cuba.

Of particular importance to women, especially those with fertility issues, Oshun remains a powerful force today.

If it is appropriate for you to work with Oshun, then she is a particular deity of love. She is represented as a lovely woman dressed in gold with a pot of honey at her waist and, often, a mirror. The colors traditionally associated with her are yellow, gold, coral, and amber, and she is also linked with the number five, as well as with honey, sunflowers, oranges, cinnamon, and pumpkin. She is associated with the peacock, like the Greek Hera, and with the vulture. Her day is Thursday.

It is said that offerings made to Oshun on the shores of rivers have particular importance. You may therefore wish to consider making an offering of honey or peacock feathers, white wine, cowrie shells, kola nuts, oranges, or coral beads before your handfasting. You can light yellow candles to her. As with all deities and spirits, it is crucial to treat her with respect, and do not underestimate her powers: there is a school of thought that says that the love goddesses of this world can create more havoc than the war goddesses. Love is a powerful force, and to be respected!

Qetesh

Qetesh is also a Canaanite goddess dating from the Bronze Age, and the center of her worship was Qadesh in what is now Syria. Like Astarte, she therefore has ancient antecedents. She is often depicted standing on a lion; in one hand, she bears a snake, and in the other, a bunch of lotuses. She is often syncretized with Astarte. She is known as "Mistress of All the Gods," "Lady of the Stars of Heaven," "Great of Magic, Mistress of the Stars," and other beautiful epithets. As a fertility goddess of ecstasy and sexual love, she, like Astarte, is also a good choice to invoke for a handfasting ceremony. You may wish to honor her in your handfasting with the symbol of the lotus or by placing lilies upon your altar.

Rati

Rati (Sanskrit: रति) is Kamadeva's consort and a goddess of lust, passion, and infatuation. She is said to be the originator of many sexual terms, some of which are found in the *Kama Sutra*, but she is portrayed as a maiden—a voluptuous and beautiful one. She is created from the sweat of Daksha, one of the sons of Lord Brahma. Some texts say that with Kamadeva, she has two children, Joy and Grace, but she has many adventures of her own, both with and without her husband. Again, remember that she is part of the living tradition of Hinduism, but should you wish to honor her during your hand-fasting, you can do so by placing flowers on your altar.

Sjofn

Mentioned in the *Prose Edda of Snorri Sturluson*, Sjofn is another Norse deity of love. The *Prose Edda* tells us that she induces both men and women to fall in love. However, we do not know much about her! Perhaps the author of the Prose Edda made her up … or she may be based on Freya.

Tu'er Shen

If you are a member of the LGBT community, you may like to invoke the blessing of the Chinese deity Tu'er Shen (Chinese: 兔兒神, the Leveret Spirit), or Rabbit God. This rabbit/hare deity looks after gay couples. His origins lie in an eighteenth-century text *The Indescribable*. Also known as *Zi Bu Yu*, or *What the Master Would Not Describe*, this is a collection of stories written by Qing scholar Yuan Muzhi, and the story of the rabbit god begins with the story of Hu Tian Bao, a young man in Fu Jian province who falls in love with a handsome imperial anticorruption officer. Hu basically stalks this man, who eventually confronts him—and when Hu reveals his love, the officer tragically slays him.

Down in the underworld, however, Hu's spirit finds that the lords of the dead are sympathetic. They ask Hu if he would like to become a rabbit god and look after gay people, and Hu complies. Appearing to a relative in a dream, he explains this, and his family build a shrine to him. He is still popular, particularly in Taiwan and Southeast Asia, and there have been drag performances dedicated to him. He is more a god of gay men than lesbians. His symbol is the rabbit, and you might like to place a little figure of a rabbit on your handfasting altar if you choose to honor him within your ceremony.

Yue Lao

Yue Lao (Chinese: 月老), or Yue Xia Lao Ren, is a Chinese god of love and marriage who appears to people under the light of the moon. His name means "the old man of the moon," and he takes the form of a wise old gentleman with a long white beard and yellow imperial robes. He carries a red cord with which he binds together couples—like the handfasting cord itself.

One of the stories of Yue Lao (there are various versions) is that during the Tang dynasty, a young man named Wei Gu was walking down the street where he saw an old man reading a book. The book turned out to be a book of marriages and engagements, and Yue Lao—for it was he—explained to the young man that he was in charge of such matters. He pointed to a little girl walking down the road and explained that this was Wei Gu's own destined bride: they would be married in the next few years. Horrified by this, Wei Gu threw a stone at the little girl, which hit her between the eyes. (In some versions of the story, he even hires a servant to stab her—for the little girl is the daughter of a blind market seller and thus too low-class for the higher-status Wei Gu. Fortunately in this version, the servant is only partially successful.)

Rather than receiving some kind of divine punishment for this, however, Wei Gu went on to be a well-respected government official working for the local governor. In the fullness of time, due to the efficiency with which he carried out his duties, the governor offered Wei Gu his own daughter in marriage. Beautiful and sweet as she was, Wei Gu readily accepted. However, his bride always wore a scarf over her head, and it was only on the wedding night that she removed it, revealing a little scar. Someone had thrown a stone at her when she was a child, she explained. Horrified all over again, Wei Gu gave sincere apologies and begged for her forgiveness, but his bride said that the circumstances were clearly strange and had obviously come about as the result of some celestial being. Thus the legend of Yue Lao spread.

Yue Lao is still popular today, and young lovers call upon him for aid: they may wear a red thread around their wrists, symbolizing the red cord that is carried by the god of love himself. The silky red string itself symbolizes a Chinese idiom, roughly translated as "a fated match across a thousand miles drawn by a thread." Two people can be destined to marry each other even though they live a thousand miles apart. You might choose to wear such a red thread during your ceremony, if you are working with this deity—but as with others above, be aware that he is a god within a living religious tradition. There is a large temple to him in Singapore, for instance, and he is also among the hundred or so deities honored in the Longshan temple in Taipei, dedicated to the Buddhist, Taoist, and Confucian communities. People petitioning the god bring sweets, since he is said to have a sweet tooth, and tie a red thread around his statue to gain his blessing on their love affairs.

Venus

The goddess Venus is essentially the Roman counterpart to the Greek Aphrodite (the Latin noun *Venus* means "sexual desire / sexual love"), but like many deities of the Classical world and elsewhere, by the time she was adopted by the Romans, the goddess had accrued other attributes. As well as being a goddess of love, she is also a goddess of fertility, victory, and prostitution. The origins of the Roman Venus lie in war, however.

In 217 BCE, as Rome was in the process of losing the Second Punic War, the Sibylline oracle suggested that Rome could win the war if the allegiance of Venus Eyrcina (Venus of Eryx) could be switched to the Romans from Carthage's Sicilian allies. Venus Eyrcina is possibly a form of Astarte.

The Romans took the goddess's image back to Rome, promising her a new and lovely temple. Thus Venus Genetrix (Venus the Mother) has her origins in the Venus of Eryx. Worshipped initially by the upper echelons of society, the cults of Venus Eycina and Venus Verticordia (Venus the Changer of Hearts) started to change and become more inclusive, and lower classes began to worship Venus Genetrix, too.

But the goddess remained popular among Rome's emperors, who were keen to retain her favor. In 55 BCE, Pompey set up a big new temple to Venus Victrix—Venus of Victory. Julius Caesar honored Venus Victrix and Venus Genetrix, claiming that both aspects of the goddess favored him: he also claimed that he was a descendent of Venus, linking this to a Roman myth that she was the mother of the Roman state through her son, the Greek hero Aeneas, who was said in popular culture to have founded Rome after the Trojan War. He is guided to Latium, the site on which Rome was founded, by Venus in the form of the morning star, shining brightly in the sky. In 139 AD, Hadrian dedicated a temple to Venus and Roma Aeterna (Eternal Rome), thus establishing Venus as the protective mother figure of the Roman state.

In 295 BCE, a temple was established to Venus Obsequens (Obedient Venus) on the Aventine Hill—allegedly funded from fines placed on Roman women for breaking sexual laws.

These are only a few of the forms of Venus that we find throughout the Roman world. Like many major deities, she is syncretized with more minor entities, foreign goddesses, and perhaps local spirits. She is heavily politicized, with many emperors claiming her favor.

You can honor Venus in your handfasting with offerings of roses, myrtle, and wine (perhaps tinctured with myrtle oil). There is a lovely ritual, Roman in origin, called the Night Watch of Venus, which culminates in a gift of roses. The ritual begins:

> *Let him love tomorrow who has never loved and let he who has loved love tomorrow.*
> *New spring, singing spring! The world is born in spring!*
> *Loves harmonize in spring, birds marry in spring,*
> *And the forest releases a marriage shower of leaves.*
> *Tomorrow the union of loves among arboreal shades*
> *interweaves lively youths in a cottage with her myrtle vine:*
> *Tomorrow Dione, propped upon her lofty throne, declares the laws.*
> *Let him love tomorrow who has never loved and let he who has loved love tomorrow.*[51]

If you are planning a handfasting in April or May, the Night Watch of Venus would be a beautiful ritual to do a few days before the ceremony. If you follow a general pagan path, then Venus and Aphrodite are the main Classical deities to approach for love magic or honoring during your handfasting. You might like to explore some of the associations that both these goddesses have: they are both syncretized with other deities, and you may resonate more with certain aspects than with others.

---

51. David Camden, trans., "Night Watch of Venus," accessed November 3, 2020, http://www.forumromanum.org/literature/pervigiliume.html.

The main festivals of Venus are held in the spring, the time when fertility begins to take hold. I have noted some of them already:

April 1: The Veneralia in honor of Venus Verticordia and Fortuna Virilis (a goddess of fortune who is probably older). This festival was focused on the purity of love and the need to adhere to the sexual proprieties.

April 23: Vinalia Urbana (a wine festival in honor of both Venus, goddess of profane wine, and Jupiter). Upper-class women would make a libation of wine; lower-class girls and prostitutes would gather at a different temple and offer mint, myrtle, and bunches of rushes and roses to the goddess in an effort to gain her favor and protection.

August 10: Vinalia Rusticia (the oldest festival dedicated to Venus in her form as Venus Obsequens). Here, Venus is a garden goddess, and kitchen and market gardens are dedicated to her. A lamb was sacrificed in her honor.

September 26: The festival of Venus Genetrix, the mother and protector of Rome.

Roman brides-to-be offered Venus a gift before the wedding, and you might like to consider doing the same.

In late antiquity, Venus was sometimes seen as a mixture of male and female, and she was sometimes depicted as being bald (like the priests of Isis in nearby Egypt). I have already mentioned the Bearded Aphrodite. The name "Venus" is masculine in origin. If you or your partner is transgender, you may wish to consider working with this archetype.

Incense and Oils for the Love Deities

With all incenses, the ingredients should be mixed in a small bowl. If you have large lumps of the resins, you will need a pestle and mortar to break them down: you need small lumps and a small quantity of powder, which will be produced by the grinding process. Incense should be a little bit moist and sticky to the touch; some incenses are very dry, but you can rectify this by adding a few drops of essential oil or a small quantity of honey.

With magical oils, you will need a carrier base, such as almond or sunflower oil, then add a few drops of the relevant essential oil. The aim of producing a magical oil is not necessarily to create something that is very fragrant: the intent behind the oil is more important than its actual scent.

Incense for Venus: 1

3 tablespoons myrrh

1 tablespoon frankincense

2 tablespoons rose petals

1 teaspoon verbena

¼ teaspoon mint

3 drops rose oil

Incense for Venus: 2

3 tablespoons frankincense

2 teaspoons sandalwood (white)

2 teaspoons rose petals

3 drops synthetic musk oil

Agrippa's Incense for Venus

1 teaspoon musk

1 teaspoon ambergris

½ teaspoon lignum aloes

3 teaspoons red rose petals

Red coral

Sparrow brain

Pigeon blood

[The last three might be a bit tricky to find, so I suggest substituting a teaspoon of red sandalwood and a pinch of dragon's blood resin.]

Incense for Aphrodite

3 tablespoons frankincense

2 teaspoons sandalwood (white)

2 teaspoons rose petals

1 teaspoon dittany of Crete

Aphrodite Oil

Almond oil base

3 drops rose oil

3 drops sandalwood oil

2 drops dittany oil

Venus Oil

Sunflower oil base

3 drops rose oil

2 drops verbena oil

Sprig of mint

Incense for Blodeuwedd

3 tablespoons frankincense

2 teaspoons dog rose

2 teaspoons broom flowers

2 teaspoons meadowsweet

1 teaspoon oak leaf

Oil for Blodeuwedd

Almond oil base

3 drops rose oil

Sprig of meadowsweet

Sprig of broom flower

Oak leaf

[Due to the unavailability of most of these herbs as essential oils, this oil is more of an infusion: use the actual leaves. Place the oil to steep in the light of the full moon to honor Blodeuwedd's darker "owl" nature.]

Incense for Freya

2 tablespoons frankincense

2 teaspoons lime blossom (the linden is sacred to Freya)

2 teaspoons cowslip flowers

2 teaspoons lady's mantle

½ teaspoon crushed amber resin

Oil for Freya

Almond oil base

3 drops lime oil

2 drops strawberry essence (the strawberry is sacred to Freya in some
modern pagan traditions)

2 drops rose oil

Incense for Hathor

1 teaspoon orrisroot

2 teaspoons myrrh

1 teaspoon sweet flag (calamus)

9 drops henna oil (from the plant's flower)

4 teaspoons rose petals

2 teaspoons spikenard

6 drops civet oil

Oil for Hathor

Sunflower oil base

3 drops myrrh oil

3 drops rose oil

2 drops civet oil

Love-Drawing Incense

3 tablespoons frankincense

2 tablespoons myrrh

3 teaspoons rose petals

1 teaspoon jasmine flowers

½ teaspoon sandalwood (white)

5 drops rose oil

Love-Drawing Oil

Almond oil base

3 drops rose oil

3 drops jasmine oil

2 drops sandalwood oil

A few rose petals

Conclusion

The gods and goddesses whom we have looked at are just a few of the love deities found around the world. It is worth considering the history of your own location and the deities that are associated with it (with the caveats I've mentioned regarding cultural appropriation: if in doubt, speak to a practitioner of the tradition in question, when possible). Hopefully, this list of deities of love and marriage will give you some ideas regarding deities to work with in your handfasting and at the beginning of your marriage. You may wish to "sign up" with a patron deity for your marriage, such as Hera, and work with them beyond the actual ceremony. This association may also be useful in relation to some of the offerings and decorations for your day. Floral decorations of mint and roses would be suitable for a summer handfasting, for instance, and these are sacred to Venus. When we come to consider the use of flowers in marriage ceremonies, we will see that there are some ancient resonances.

Chapter Twelve
The Language of Flowers

The language of flowers is quite an old one. The idea that every flower has a symbolic meaning has been with us for a long time and perhaps reached its peak in the Victorian period, when women would buy "flower dictionaries" outlining the meaning of flowers. Victorian women would often carry little bouquets called tussie-mussies consisting of flowers that could, together, convey a message to those in the know.

For instance, a bride might carry a bouquet of roses (love), baby's breath (love everlasting), and ferns (sincerity). Many of us have lost the knowledge of the language of flowers, but a lot of florists are aware of it and can advise you, or you may wish to do some research of your own. In this chapter, we will look at the magic of flowers and how they can be incorporated into your own handfasting ceremony.

The History of the Language of Flowers

Jayne Alcock, grounds and gardens supervisor at the Walled Gardens of Cannington, says that the language of flowers has its origins in Ottoman Turkey.[52]

This interest in floriography, as it is known, was introduced to Europe by Englishwoman Mary Wortley Montagu (1689–1762), who took it to England in 1717. Aubry de La Mottraye (1674–1743) introduced it to the Swedish

---

52. Jayne Alcock, *The Language of Flowers* (Bridgwater: Bridgwater College, 2016).

court in 1727. We shall see below that the royal families of both England and Sweden carry on this tradition in their wedding bouquets.

The *Dictionnaire du Langage des Fleurs* by Joseph Hammer-Purgstall is the first known published list of the flowers with their meanings. The first dictionary of floriography, *Le Langage des Fleurs*, was written by Louise Cortambert (under the pen name Madame Charlotte de la Tour). Such was the popularity of the idea that many subsequent books were produced, including *The Language of Flowers*, illustrated by Kate Greenaway, and Henry Phillips's *Floral Emblems*. Floriography was immensely popular not only in Britain, but also in Europe and the US. Catharine H. Waterman Esling's poem titled "The Language of Flowers" appeared in her own language of flowers book, *Flora's Lexicon*, in 1839.

Although floriography has mostly gone out of fashion in everyday life, one area where it is still going strong is in the floral arrangements for wedding ceremonies. Let's look at some bouquets carried by the royal families of Europe, as this is where this old language of flowers is probably still consciously and ritually used. You might like to use some of these bouquets as inspiration for your own handfasting.

There are several constant motifs in royal weddings in Britain: orange blossom was used for floral wreaths from Queen Victoria onward, the floral symbols of the nations of the UK are also often used, and myrtle (which is sacred to Venus) is a traditional part of royal bouquets.

Designed by Shane Connolly, Kate Middleton's wedding bouquet at her marriage to Prince William contained a combination of symbolic flowers: lilies (return of happiness), hyacinths (steady love), ivy (fidelity and friendship), and myrtle, a symbol of matrimony, which is traditionally always included in the bouquets carried by royal brides in Britain and is usually cut from a bush at Osborne House, Queen Victoria's residence on the Isle of Wight. The bodice of the Duchess's dress was embroidered with roses, thistles, and shamrocks, which represent England, Scotland, and Ireland.

Meghan Markle, too, carried a sprig of myrtle, along with sweet peas, lily of the valley, astilbe, jasmine, and astrantia. The bouquet included forget-me-nots, handpicked by Prince Harry from the private garden at Kensington Palace. These were his mother Princess Diana's favorite flowers. Again, the flowers chosen by Meghan were not just those she carried in her bouquet: her sixteen-and-a-half-foot silk tulle veil was hand embroidered with flowers representing the fifty-three countries of the Commonwealth, plus the California poppy, representing Meghan's home state, and wintersweet, which apparently grows in the garden of the couple's first marital home, Nottingham Cottage.

Diana herself, in 1981, carried a bouquet from the Worshipful Company of Gardeners that contained the following flowers:

- Gardenias
- Stephanotis
- Orchid
- Lily of the valley
- Earl Mountbatten roses
- Freesia
- Veronica
- Ivy
- Myrtle
- Tradescantia

Diana's bouquet was designed and created by Longman's florists in London, like that of the Queen for her own wedding in 1947, when she was still Princess Elizabeth. However, Her Majesty's bouquet actually went missing—Longman's had to hastily produce another one (and having learned from experience, they produced a stunt double for Diana's bouquet, just in case!). The bouquet included orchids: cattleya, cypripedium, and odontoglossum, all British-grown. Princess Elizabeth's duchesse satin gown also had floral symbolism: the motifs of star lilies and orange blossom, which were apparently inspired by Botticelli's Primavera to symbolize rebirth after the devastation of World War II.

Also following tradition, the Duchess of Cambridge's bridal bouquet was laid at the Grave of the Unknown Warrior inside Westminster Abbey after the wedding.

In the US, Jacqueline Bouvier married Senator John F. Kennedy in Newport, Rhode Island, and she carried a bouquet of white and pink gardenias plus white orchids and stephanotis.

All of these are examples of the language of flowers—used today in weddings among the great houses of Europe and elsewhere. This is a custom that can be personalized to you: flowers that have a specific meaning to you, or that represent the county, place, town, or state from which you come, can be used for your handfasting bouquet or decorations. If you're from Massachusetts, for example, you might consider trailing arbutus as part of your bouquet, or yucca flowers if you come from New Mexico. Teleflora have an "official" list of state flowers, as follows. The 1893 World's Fair in Chicago encouraged states to choose their own emblematic flower (several were selected by school children), and many of these are still linked to the relevant states today. Many others are over a hundred years old:

United States

Alabama: Camellia

Alaska: Forget-me-not

Arizona: Saguaro cactus blossom

Arkansas: Apple blossom

California: California poppy

Colorado: Rocky Mountain columbine

Connecticut: Mountain laurel

Delaware: Peach blossom

Florida: Orange blossom

Georgia: Cherokee rose

Hawaii: Hibiscus

Idaho: Mock orange

Illinois: Purple violet

Indiana: Peony

Iowa: Wild prairie rose

Kansas: Sunflower

Kentucky: Goldenrod

Louisiana: Magnolia

Maine: White pine tassel and cone

Maryland: Black-eyed Susan

Massachusetts: Mayflower

Michigan: Apple blossom

Minnesota: Pink and white lady's slipper

Mississippi: Magnolia

Missouri: Hawthorn

Montana: Bitterroot

Nebraska: Goldenrod

Nevada: Sagebrush

New Hampshire: Purple lilac

New Jersey: Violet

New Mexico: Yucca ("Lamparas de Dios"/Lamps of the Lord)

New York: Rose

North Carolina: Flowering dogwood

North Dakota: Wild prairie rose

Ohio: Scarlet carnation

Oklahoma: Mistletoe

Oregon: Oregon grape

Pennsylvania: Mountain laurel

Rhode Island: Violet

South Carolina: Yellow jessamine

South Dakota: Pasqueflower

Tennessee: Iris

Texas: Texas bluebonnet

Utah: Sego lily

Vermont: Red clover

Virginia: Flowering dogwood

Washington: Coast rhododendron

West Virginia: Rhododendron

Wisconsin: Violet

Wyoming: Indian paintbrush

British counties also have official flowers, and you can find a list for your own county below. In the case of the UK, this list only dates from the olden days of 2002, when there was a national competition to assign flowers to each county. This generated some controversy, as some counties were already strongly associated with flowers, such as Yorkshire, traditionally linked with the white rose (remember the Wars of the Roses) but newly assigned the harebell. However, though you might like to take this seriously for magical reasons, it's not worth going to war over!

England

Bedfordshire: Bee orchid

Berkshire: Summer snowflake

Birmingham: Foxglove

Bristol: Maltese-cross

Buckinghamshire: Chiltern gentian

Cambridgeshire: Pasqueflower

Cheshire: Cuckooflower

Cornwall/Kernow: Cornish heath

Cumberland: Grass of Parnassus

Derbyshire: Jacob's ladder

Devon: Primrose

Dorset: Dorset heath

County Durham: Spring gentian

Essex: Poppy

Gloucestershire: Wild daffodil

Hampshire: Dog rose

Herefordshire: Mistletoe

Hertfordshire: Pasqueflower

Huntingdonshire: Water violet

Isle of Man: Fuchsia

Isle of Wight: Pyramidal orchid

Isles of Scilly: Thrift

Kent: Hop

Lancashire: Red rose

Leeds: Bilberry

Leicestershire: Foxglove

Lincolnshire: Common dog violet

Liverpool: Sea holly

London: Rosebay willowherb

Manchester: Common cottongrass

Middlesex: Wood anemone

Newcastle-upon-Tyne: Monkeyflower

Norfolk: Alexanders

Northamptonshire: Cowslip

Northumberland: Bloody crane's-bill

Nottingham: Nottingham catchfly

Nottinghamshire: Autumn crocus

Oxfordshire: Fritillary

Rutland: Clustered bellflower

Sheffield: Wood crane's-bill

Shropshire: Round-leaved sundew

Somerset: Cheddar pink

Staffordshire: Heather

Suffolk: Oxlip

Surrey: Cowslip

Sussex: Round-headed rampion

Warwickshire: Honeysuckle

Westmoreland: Alpine forget-me-not

Wiltshire: Burnt orchid

Worcestershire: Cowslip

Yorkshire: Harebell

Northern Ireland

Antrim: Harebell

Armagh: Cowbane

Belfast: Gorse

Derry: Purple saxifrage

Down: Spring squill

Fermanagh: Globeflower

Tyrone: Bog rosemary

Scotland

Aberdeenshire: Bearberry

Angus/Forfarshire: Alpine catchfly

Argyllshire: Foxglove

Ayrshire: Green-winged orchid

Banffshire: Dark-red helleborine

Berwickshire: Rock-rose

Buteshire: Thrift

Caithness: Scottish primrose

Clackmannanshire: Opposite-leaved golden saxifrage

Cromartyshire: Spring cinquefoil

Dumfriesshire: Harebell

Dunbartonshire: Lesser water-plantain

East Lothian/Haddingtonshire: Viper's bugloss

Edinburgh: Sticky catchfly

Fife: Coralroot orchid

Glasgow: Broom

Inverness-shire: Twinflower

Kinross-shire: Holy grass

Kirkcudbrightshire: Bog-rosemary

Lanarkshire: Dune helleborine

Morayshire: One-flowered wintergreen

Nairnshire: Chickweed wintergreen

Orkney: Alpine bearberry

Peebles-shire: Cloudberry

Perthshire: Alpine gentian

Renfrewshire: Bogbean

Ross-shire: Bog asphodel

Roxburghshire: Maiden pink

Selkirkshire: Mountain pansy

Shetland: Shetland mouse-ear

Stirlingshire: Scottish dock

Sutherland: Grass of Parnassus

Western Isles: Hebridean spotted-orchid

West Lothian/Linlithgowshire: Common spotted-orchid

Wigtownshire: Yellow iris

Wales

Anglesey/Sir Fon: Spotted rock-rose

Brecknockshire/Sir Frycheiniog: Cuckooflower

Caernarvonshire/Sir Gaernarfon: Snowdon lily

Cardiff/Caerdydd: Wild leek

Cardiganshire/Ceredigion: Bog rosemary

Carmarthenshire/Sir Gaerfyddin: Whorled caraway

Denbighshire/Sir Ddinbych: Limestone woundwort

Flintshire/Sir Fflint: Bell heather

Glamorgan/Morgannwg: Yellow whitlow-grass

Merioneth/Merionnydd: Welsh poppy

Monmouthshire/Sir Fynwy: Foxglove

Montgomeryshire/Sir Drefaldwyn: Spiked speedwell

Pembrokeshire/Sir Benfro: Thrift

Radnorshire/Sir Faesyfed: Radnor lily

If you're an embroiderer or you know someone who is, it's a nice idea to incorporate some of this floral symbolism into a dress or cloak. You can ask a florist to make up your specific bouquet (and most of them like a challenge!), or you can do what one young couple in the South West of England did and grow all the flowers for your bouquet yourself. They spent a year growing poppies, dahlias, sweet peas, and wildflowers, including blue cornflowers, and did all the wedding floral arrangements themselves, using the flowers for bouquets, table arrangements, and a floral arch. The flowers decorated the buttonholes of the groomsmen's suits, and the confetti was made out of dried petals. After this, some friends asked them to grow flowers for their own weddings, too.

This is quite an undertaking, and no one would expect you to go that far! But it is definitely worth thinking about the symbolism of your flowers: they can be a big part of a ceremony.

Here are some flowers and their meanings. Be a bit careful with a few flowers—orange lilies signify hatred, for example! Sweet peas and cyclamen mean "farewell," yellow carnations signify disappointment, and striped ones mean a refusal. Foxgloves signify insincerity, and daffodils refer to unrequited love. You might want to consider excluding these from your bouquet—although I would say that if they are your favorite flowers, you should go ahead.

Alstroemeria: Devotion and friendship
Alyssum: Worth beyond beauty
Anemone: Unfading love
Apple Blossom: Good fortune
Artemisia: Dignity
Baby's Breath: Everlasting love
Calla Lily: Magnificent beauty
Camellia: Perfected loveliness
Carnation: Pride and beauty, fascination
Chrysanthemums (White): Truth
Daisy: Innocence
Forget-Me-Not: Memories
Gardenia: Secret love
Gladioli: Sincerity
Heather (Pink): Good luck
Jasmine: Cheer and grace

Jonquil: Desire

Lilac: First sign of love

Lily: Purity of heart

Lily (White): Purity and sweetness

Lily of the Valley: Return of happiness

Orange Blossom: Marriage and fruitfulness

Orchid: Beauty

Peony: Shame or happy marriage

Queen Anne's Lace: Fantasy

Red Rose: Passionate love

Rudbeckia: Justice

Sunflower: Adoration

Tulips (Red): Love

Violet: Modesty and "you occupy my thoughts"

Yellow Daylilies: Coquetry

Zinnia (Burgundy): Lasting affection

Zinnia (Mixed): Thoughts of absent friends

Flowers can be used in ways other than in your bouquet for your hand-fasting. A wreath for your hair is a lovely adornment, and you can also decorate the venue with appropriate flowers: either ones that are chosen for their meanings, or ones that represent the season in which you are holding your handfasting ceremony—I have suggested corn for Lughnasadh, for instance, or snowdrops at Imbolc. You might want to use your bouquet as an offering, perhaps placing it on your altar (leaving anything behind in a sacred space is not usually a good idea, but you could place it beneath a tree in your garden as an offering to the gods, for instance).

You could also dry the petals and use them in an incense. Making your own handfasting incense is a custom that is followed by many couples, and you might want to include some appropriate flowers along with resins, such as frankincense and pine.

Petals make great confetti, are usually ecologically sound, and in some countries are traditional (the Greeks throw rice and rose petals over the couple at weddings, for example). Throwing confetti as a good wish for the handfasting couple can be considered a magical act, particularly if you follow the language of flowers. Barley is traditional in Sicily if you want a baby boy, or wheat for a baby girl. Turmeric-spiced rice is thrown at Hindu weddings—but you might want to avoid this if you are wearing white! Greek weddings may feature decorative bundles of *koufeta*: these contain an indivisible prime number (3, 5, 7, 11), symbolizing that the couple will never be divided.

Conclusion

Flowers are a classic symbol of love and marriage, and there is a strong pagan element to their use in handfasting ceremonies. The language of flowers is not specifically pagan, but according to the theory of correspondences, plants, herbs, trees, and flowers all have a place in magical traditions. Each one has a meaning and a significance in ritual magic, which can be incorporated into your handfasting in a particularly beautiful way. Quite apart from this, it's also meaningful to have your favorite flowers adorning your ceremony!

Chapter Thirteen
Herbs for Handfasting

Let's say that you want to carry out a love spell to ensure the success of your marriage—and in its purest form, a handfasting is just that! The information in this chapter is based on the theory of correspondences, on which so much magical practice is based.

The theory of correspondences is an old concept. We find it used in magic across the ancient world, from Egypt, to Greece and Rome, to name but a few places. As we've noted elsewhere, the theory is based on the notion that objects and ideas, which may not closely resemble one another, are nonetheless connected on a metaphysical or some kind of subconscious level. This link means that magical practitioners can use these objects and ideas to bring about a particular result. We're going to be looking at some correspondences: the herbs that are most closely related to love in the ancient traditions of the Western world. Some of these are sacred to Venus herself, and some are sacred to other gods and goddesses, to other planets and stars, but all are still nonetheless linked to love.

You can use the correspondences in a variety of ways in your own handfasting:

- Incense
- Oil
- Bouquet
- Garlands

- Confetti (The ancient Greeks and Romans threw grains or seeds—this is nice, but remember to check whether it's appropriate to throw seeds that might grow in an ecologically sensitive location. Might be food for the birds, though!)

I'll be looking into the properties of the following herbs:

- Dittany of Crete
- Basil
- Calendula
- Coltsfoot
- Lavender
- Mint
- Patchouli
- Red clover
- Rose
- Rosemary
- Vervain
- Yarrow

You can purchase these herbs from health food stores (either online or in person), witchcraft or esoteric suppliers, or garden centers. You may like to grow your own if you have a garden or other outside space, such as a balcony.

Dittany of Crete (*Origanum dictamnus*)

Dittany has very ancient roots as a magical herb. As its Latin name suggests, it is a member of the oregano family and originates in Greece. The name is complex: *origanum* means both "joy" and "mountains," whereas *dictamnus* refers to the birthplace of Zeus—*Dikti* relates to the mountain and *thamnos* means "shrub." The plant was said to be given to the island of Crete after it sheltered Zeus's mother, Rhea. But it has associations with a number of Greek deities—Aphrodite is said to have used its healing properties to treat Aeneas at the war of Troy; thus it is linked with love magic as well as healing. Statues of Artemis were crowned with dittany, and Diktynna, an early

Minoan goddess also known as Britomartis, has left her name across the island—including the mountain after which the herb is partially named. Diktynna was a maiden pursued by King Minos, but she evaded his clutches and sought refuge with the virgin goddess Artemis, who granted her immortality in reward for her purity.

At your handfasting, you can scatter dittany to bring you luck in love.

Basil (*Ocimum basilicum*)

Also called "sweet basil," basil belongs to the mint family. Its name comes from the Greek *basilikos*, which means "herb worthy of a king." It used to be associated with hatred in early times (perhaps because it is said to be of use in dispelling demonic powers!), but later, in Italy, it became linked with love. The Romans maintained that it was sacred to Venus and thus ideal for use in love magic.

Calendula (*Calendula officinalis*)

Its name comes from the Latin *Calends*, referring to the first day of the summer months in the Roman calendar; it was supposed to flower on this day. In folklore, you are supposed to pick it when the Sun enters the sign of Virgo. As a solar herb, it minimizes the power of the energy of Mars and balances and calms aggression. To utilize its protective qualities during your handfasting, a few petals can be kept in a white bag about your person and held to receive the sun's warming, healing qualities, or you can make some calendula ointment to anoint yourself and perhaps your bridesmaids to bring its healing properties into your handfasting ceremony.

Calendula Ointment

500 milliliters infused marigold oil
40 grams cocoa butter
40 grams yellow beeswax

Warm the oil (do not boil). Melt the cocoa butter and beeswax until you have a smooth ointment. Cool and store in glass jars. You may like to give this as favors to special people in your summer handfasting.

Coltsfoot (*Tussilago farfara*)

Coltsfoot is held to increase psychic awareness in conjunction with other "psychic development" herbs, such as angelica or dittany, and it is said that smoking coltsfoot can produce visions (I don't recommend this, although it is an ingredient in some herbal smoking mixes). Being dedicated to Venus and to the element of water, it is also used in love magic. If you're getting married in the early spring, look out for coltsfoot and perhaps include it in your bouquet.

Lavender (*Lavandula angustifolia*)

Lavender is one of the great cleansers and an essential and familiar part of the kitchen garden. Along with mint and rosemary, it's a cleanser and a protector. It's linked to the element of air and to Mercury.

Lavender is also used in love magic and to attract money. It can be used in a small bag as a charm to draw prosperity toward oneself. With rosemary and placed in a little bag, lavender can be used to protect one's chastity—this was more relevant in medieval times than nowadays, but more seriously, one can still use this as a means of protecting one's personal space! In your handfasting, this probably isn't necessary—but you can scatter lavender flowers or make lavender water to sprinkle about the handfasting space in order to purify it.

Mint (*Mentha*)

Mint is one of the most popular herbs in the British tradition, and as anyone who has a garden knows, once some of its many varieties are in the ground, it's almost impossible to get rid of! However, that might be a good thing, as it has so many positive uses in both medicinal herbalism and magical practice. In ancient Athens, mint was woven into bridal garlands along with marigolds, so it has a long association with marriage, and you might want to consider mint, with its fresh aroma, for your handfasting.

Magically, its use is ancient: it was part of the sacred drink in the Eleusinian Mysteries, and peppermint has been found in Egyptian tombs. Pliny recommends wearing a crown of mint to aid mental processes, and it is possible that its name comes from the Latin *mente*, or "thought." It can be used, therefore, to sharpen concentration in ritual or to cleanse the mind—its oil can be used in ritual baths, and if you are intending to undertake any purification rituals prior to your handfasting, you might like to consider adding a sprig of mint.

Patchouli (*Pogostemon cablin*)

Patchouli is a member of the mint family and, to many people, will be a reminder of the 1960s with its characteristically musky scent. It is often associated with love magic and can, when dried, be placed in a pillow to perfume your room or the handfasting space. You can scatter its leaves around the handfasting circle or burn them in an oil burner during the ceremony to perfume your handfasting.

Rose (*Rosa*)

The rose, in its many forms, has been a flower symbolizing love for many years. Rose water and attar of roses have been staple perfumes throughout the Middle East and, later, medieval Britain.

In aromatherapy, rose is used as a calming, soothing oil. It is also used as a symbol throughout the royal houses of Britain—the white and red roses—and is the national symbol of England itself. Thus, its qualities extend beyond love magic into a symbol of the goddess of sovereignty herself.

There is a Greek legend that the rose was formed from the body of a dead nymph whom the goddess of flowers, Chloris, found in the forest. The Three Graces enlisted the help of the other gods to turn her into a new flower and gave her joy, brilliance, and early blossoming; Dionysus gave her an intoxicating, sensual perfume; and Chloris made her queen of the flowers. This emergence from death into new life gives us a hint of the darker aspect of love: the underworld aspect of Venus. In the *Iliad*, Hector's body is anointed with rose oil after his death.

There are other stories: white roses are supposed to come from the seafoam that scattered from Aphrodite as she emerged from the waves. When she attempts to help the wounded Adonis, a drop of blood changes the white rose to red.

Victorian women used to dip rose petals in sugar and dry them in the oven, then give them as gifts to their suitors: a genteel kind of love magic! But rose petals are used in all manner of love spells—in incense, potpourri, or charms (hang some in a small bag around your neck) to attract love, or in a massage oil with sandalwood as an aphrodisiac. Cleopatra was said to have washed the sails of her ship with rose water to herald her arrival.

The beautiful rose is often used in handfastings; it's a classic wedding flower, and for a summer handfasting, you may wish to include it in your bouquet, or as a wreath for your hair, or in the decorations.

Rosemary (*Rosemarinus officinalis*)

Rosemary's name comes from the Latin *ros marinus*, or "sea dew."

Along with mint, rosemary is another of the great purifiers and also a good cleanser of mind, spirit, and space. Magically, it has some of the same properties as mint. Whereas mint is usually associated with the element of water, rosemary is linked to the sun, to Venus, and to fire. Rosemary, too, is protective, and it's a powerful magical cleanser. You can put a sprig of it under your pillow before your handfasting to ward off bad dreams and hang it up in the house to keep negative influences away. Like mint, it has been found in Egyptian tombs. In medieval times, it was associated with love and memory and could be thrown into graves as a sign that the dead would be remembered (as in Shakespeare's Ophelia: "Rosemarie, that's for remembrance ...").

Greek scholars are said to have worn a sprig of the herb as an aid to mental concentration and intellectual acuity. It is another good herb to use before your ceremony as a cleanser and during ritual (or outside it) as a protective element. It has been used as a love charm for generations. Again, it's a good herb to include in handfasting bouquets or garlands.

Vervain (*Verbena officinalis*)

Vervain is one of the major magical plants, as its early names reflect (wizard's plant, enchanter's plant, and holy wort, among others). The *Druid Plant Oracle* deck tells us that on the Isle of Man, vervain was just known as "the herb," without further explanation! Pliny tells us that it was one of the four herbs used by the Druids (along with mistletoe, selago—possibly fir moss—and a plant known as "Samolus," which could be a number of things) and was correspondingly important in ancient times.

Vervain is a Druidic herb, and Pliny and the ancients say that one is supposed to gather it before the sun is up, or, more specifically, in the dark of the moon when Sirius is rising. It must be cut with a sickle and raised up with the left hand, then an offering of honeycomb should be made to the earth. In later ages, if you were to summon demons (I don't recommend that for your handfasting!), you needed to be crowned with vervain.

It was used in Roman and Greek times as a purificatory, protective herb and strewn on the altars of Zeus and Jupiter to cleanse them, as well as sprinkled over floors to purify a house from evil spirits.

In British folklore, vervain is said to staunch blood flow because it sprang up at the foot of Calvary when nails were driven into the hands of Christ. But it was also used in that old protective way—a bag containing the herb was said to protect one from nightmares (homeopaths use it as a remedy for insomnia—it seems to have protective nocturnal properties!), and the Jacobean poet Drayton mentions that it "hindreth witches in their will."[53] Presumably he is referring to the murkier kind of witch and not to our current good selves!

Frazer tells us in his book *The Golden Bough* that bunches of vervain can be cast into the fire on Saint John's Eve (June 23) to cast out bad luck—again, the plant has a strongly protective theme, and you can use it as an element of a purifying bath before your handfasting, or scatter its leaves around the circle. Its connections with Midsummer go back a long way, as it is harvested at this time of year.

Vervain is also sacred to Venus and has a use in love spells, hence its inclusion here. This probably stems from an ancient belief that it was an aphrodisiac.

---

53. Michael Drayton, *The Folk-Lore Journal* (Abingdon, 1885), 134–155.

Yarrow (*Achillea millefolium*)

Yarrow is associated with everlasting love and is one of the most useful herbs in both the magical and the medicinal herbal arsenal. It is one of the several herbs that is known as "all-heal" because of its remarkable properties, and it has been a friend to humankind for a very long time: its pollen appears in Neanderthal graves, and the writer Pliny notes that Achilles was taught by the centaur Chiron to make a salve from yarrow to heal his injuries (hence the plant's Latin name!).

Throughout the Celtic world, yarrow is held to be a fairy herb. It is used in divinatory practices, and in love spells, and in war, so its magical applications are as wide and far-reaching as its medicinal ones (this kind of analogous working is often the case in herbal magic).

The *Druid Plant Oracle* tells us that yarrow is known in folklore as "Seven Years' Love" and that it was used in love spells to ensure fidelity. Scottish women used to pick it with their eyes shut on May Day while reciting, "Good morrow, good morrow, to thee braw yarrow. And thrice good morrow to thee. I pray tell me today or tomorrow wha' is my true love to be." In East Anglia, the yarrow was gathered at midnight, and if the dew was still on it in the morning, a girl knew she would be courted.

Bunches of yarrow were also placed on cradles to keep a baby sweet-natured, but the plant was not used as actual decoration in the home, as this was said to be unlucky.

Conclusion

Herbalism has been a part of magical practice for hundreds of years, and contemporary magic is no exception. As we have seen in this chapter, all these herbs can be used in various ways: in incense or oils, as decoration, in your handfasting bouquet, or in garlands. Their use gives you a chance to include some hands-on magical practice in the run-up to your ceremony.

Chapter Fourteen
The Ogham Trees and Handfasting

In our chapter about ritual tools, I looked at making a wand for your handfasting and mentioned that you might like to choose a particular tree out of which to make a wand: your choice might, for example, depend on your own date of birth and the tree that corresponds to this, or the time of year. As with the use of flowers, this "ties" your handfasting into the season and lends additional symbolic meaning to your ceremony.

Below, I have listed the woods most suitable for handfasting wands or decorations. Some of these trees have associations (such as the willow with funerals) that are not really appropriate for a marital ceremony, but individual practitioners may have personal links with various trees that override those associations. I have included all of them that are, for example, associated with love, marriage, or the relevant gods and goddesses.

Beth (Birch) December 24 to January 20

The beautiful birch is the first tree of the Ogham and represents new beginnings. According to myth, the first thing carved in the Ogham was carved on a birch rod. The birch tree symbolizes freshness, newness, and cleansing. It is a protective tree, long associated with the fairy realm. Its title Lady of the Woods is a good indication of this silvery, delicate tree.

It is one of the first trees to come into leaf in spring, the purplish buds giving forth bright green leaves. It is sacred to Odin's wife, Frigga, a goddess of marriage and childbirth (maybe she uses a birch besom to keep her celestial home clean!).

In Wales, giving a birch garland to someone means that you love them, and this tree seems associated throughout Celtic legend with love. Its planet is Venus, and so it's an ideal tree to use for a ceremonial handfasting wand or as decoration for your ceremony—perhaps in an arch.

Luis (Rowan) January 21 to February 17

Sometimes known as "mountain ash," the rowan is one of the best-loved British trees. With its distinctive frothy white flowers and, later in the year, its striking red or orange berries, it is a familiar sight along the slopes of the Welsh and Scottish hills and throughout the country generally.

Rowan holds a long history in folklore, from Scandinavia across to the Celtic nations, for being a tree that protects against negative magic. In one of the Irish sagas, it is described as "fid na ndruad" (the Druid's tree), and the Druids are supposed to have lit rowan fires for divinatory and protective purposes. Later, sprigs of rowan were tied above the lintels of doors to keep negative magic and evil spirits away; you may like to consider this for a handfasting arch.

Nion (Ash) February 18 to March 17

The ash is one of the most familiar trees of the British and Irish landscape, and it's easy to distinguish at close quarters due to its "hooves"—it has small black tips that resemble a cloven hoof. In Norse legend, the god Odin is supposed to have hung on an ash tree, the great "world tree" Yggdrasil, for "nine days and nine nights" in order to be given the wisdom of the runes. Odin has a nine-legged horse, the magical Sleipnir, and one cannot help wondering if the ash tree itself is his steed!

Ash has an ancient relationship with humankind, and there are legends that hold that humans are in some way descended from ash trees. The Greek goddess Nemesis carries an ash branch to mete out the justice of the gods.

In both British and Irish legend, the ash is said to "court lightning," and it's best not to stand underneath it in a thunderstorm. That suggests a difficult relationship with the element of fire, and indeed, the ash is usually considered to be a "water" tree. It can be used in rituals to honor the sea, as it was linked to the Greek/Roman god Poseidon/Neptune. If you are having a handfasting near water, or if you are born under a water sign, you might want to include this lovely tree in your decorations.

Fearn (Alder) March 18 to April 14

The alder is a wetlands tree. It often grows alongside water, sometimes with its feet in it. The wood was used for the pilings in the ancient lake villages of the Celts, because it is so tough that it can withstand being submerged in water for many years without rotting. It was also used for making shields, and thus its use in magic is chiefly protective. It makes hot charcoal and contributes to the forging of weapons.

In Greek myth, alder was connected to Cronos, the ancient lord of time. One of the names associated with him is Fearinus, the "dawn of the year," and this might have influenced the Irish name for alder, which is "fearn."

However, in the folklore of Ireland and Northern Europe, the alder has a darker reputation. The Alder King is supposed to steal children away in Danish legend, and the tree is closely associated with death. It's not necessarily a first choice for a handfasting, but you may wish to use it if you are a water sign.

Saille (Willow) April 15 to May 12

As another familiar tree in the British landscape, it should come as no surprise that willow is closely associated with the element of water. And as it is one of the first trees to stir in the year (and one of the last to lose its leaves, too), its connection with spring is appropriate.

The willow is linked with the moon, with the feminine, and with the powers of the unconscious mind. In ancient Greece, the underworld goddess Persephone had at least one shrine in groves of willow, and so did the goddess Helice—if you know your constellations, you have met her already. Jealous of her husband's infatuation with Helice, Hera, the queen of heaven, transformed Helice into the Great Bear and placed her far away in the sky.

But the greatest of the deities linked to the willow is Hecate, whose symbols also include the moon and water.

It may be because of these very early connections to willow that the tree is used in funeral customs. It is thus not ideal for a handfasting! But it is a beautiful and decorative tree, and many women in particular feel a connection with it.

Huath (Hawthorn) May 13 to June 9

The white blossom of the hawthorn, may, is still one of our surest signs of spring—the month of May is, after all, named after it! And it is connected with some of that old weather lore that our ancestors used to follow—"ne'er cast a clout till (the) may be out" is still sound advice. Yet hawthorn has a chancy reputation in British superstition—my own family, who are Welsh and Scots, were never happy about bringing flowering hawthorn into the house, feeling that it would be unlucky. If you are having a Beltane handfasting, however, the use of may is entirely appropriate.

Duir (Oak) June 10 to July 7

The oak is one of the strongest tree symbols in the British Isles. Often seen as the national tree, this powerful emblem features in a great deal of the folklore of the country. Kings hide in it. In the Welsh legends of the *Mabinogion*, Gwydion finds his missing nephew Llew Llaw Gyffes in an oak tree. Its majestic spreading branches feature on many coats of arms. Druids were said to gather mistletoe from it (although it is rare to find mistletoe on an oak tree—perhaps this is why it was so valued!).

In the Ogham, the oak symbolizes strength and power. As a royal symbol, if you draw it in a reading, it relates to your capacity to contact your inner strength and the power of the land. It is a very masculine tree. Its Irish name, Duir, refers to a door, and this is also a clue to its more hidden inner nature—it is a doorway into the realm of the spiritual—and it may be that the very name of "Druid" is related to the oak tree.

Tinne (Holly) July 8 to August 4

The Romans gave gifts of holly during their festival of Saturnalia, and there is a Christian legend that holly sprang up behind Christ's feet. There's another link in the old carol "The Holly and the Ivy," which speaks of the colors of the holly.

The Holly King fights the Oak King at Midsummer and takes over again for the darker half of the year—so the time around the summer solstice is his time, too.

It is a dream plant, and placing nine holly leaves under your pillow is said to reveal your future husband in your dreams (a bit prickly, though!). The tree generally is held to be a protector against evil magic and against lightning. Pliny mentions it in Roman times as a protective tree, so this tradition is very old. Holly keeps you safe from evil witches in Scotland, and fairies love it, so you must not mistreat it!

Holly is also linked to fire—those fiery berries! It's a good decoration for a Midwinter handfasting.

Coll (Hazel) August 5 to September 1

The hazel is one of the great magical trees in Celtic mythology, but it appears also in other mythological systems. It is the hazel whose nuts fall into the Pool of Segais and are eaten by the salmon of wisdom, one of the oldest creatures on Earth in Welsh legend. There is an Irish correlate in the story of Connla's Well, which is overlooked by "nine poetic hazels" whose nuts fall into the water and are also eaten by a salmon: bright spots manifest on his body, depending on how many nuts he eats. The well itself is said to be under the sea, or in the otherworld, and one suspects that the wisdom here is water wisdom, the innate migratory knowledge of the salmon. In Norse legend, Mimir's Well is another source of knowledge and wisdom.

Jacqueline Patterson compares the hazel leaf itself to the silvery flashing shape of a fish, and in Irish and Welsh legend, both Fionn and Taliesin gain their knowledge by eating (or just touching to their lips) the skin of a magical salmon.

The hazel, and its quicksilver appearance, is linked to Mercury. Druids legendarily carried rods of hazel, and one may see it as a divining rod for inspiration. To gather one, find a tree that has not yet borne fruit, and cut a branch at sunrise with a sickle on a Wednesday.

Muin (Vine) September 2 to September 29

Although "muin" refers to the vine, it may be more appropriate in this country to regard it as the bramble—although vines are grown here, they don't produce wonderful wine (in my opinion!). And of course, blackberries can be used in home winemaking, too. Vines are thus linked to Dionysus, the lionskin-clad god of the vine and the grape, whose abundant gifts can display a darker side if they are abused. Muin suggests that we need temporarily to bypass the rational mind and rely on the intuition and instinct. It's ideal to use vines as a theme for a happy time such as handfasting.

Gort (Ivy) September 30 to October 27

In the Ogham system of divination, ivy's coils and tendrils refer to its strength. It clings, creeps, pushes its way through concrete and brick, and although its coiling "branches" may seem delicate, the roots are often enormous, linking the ivy securely to the earth. It is hard to destroy, as anyone who has ever tried to remove it from a building will know, and it is extremely tenacious and good at living in quite desolate places.

Ngetal (Reed) October 28 to November 24

The reed is a powerful symbol within the Ogham, based on fables regarding its strength. It bends in high winds, remaining flexible and pliant, unlike bigger, more rigid trees, which are prone to topple. Liz Murray, in the *Celtic Tree Oracle*, suggests that reed refers to communication (the Eight of Wands in the tarot, with its flying staffs, has a similar meaning) and sending messages out into the wider world. She suggests that this plant is linked with finding direction.

Reeds have a long association with humankind, as they are used for so many things. In my part of the world (Somerset), we have many reed beds, and along with willow, they can be used for basket making. Once, reeds were used as thatch or as floor covering. They are also a home for many birds and water creatures, and Ngetal is sometimes linked to the goose. If you are having a handfasting at this time of year, you could hark back to medieval times and scatter rushes over the floor of your place of ritual or celebration.

Ruis (Elder) November 25 to December 22

The name comes from the Saxon *ellaern* (hollow) or *aeld* (fire), possibly because its hollow twigs were used to blow life into fires.

Ruled by Venus, elder is known as the witch's tree, and witches were supposed to be able to turn themselves into one. It is held to be unlucky and associated with evil, but it has many medicinal uses. Elder, nettle, and corncrake are supposed to be a sign of an unlucky place—presumably because they all frequent places that have been abandoned.

In some systems, December 23 is not ruled by any tree, for it is the traditional day of the proverbial "year and a day."

Conclusion

The system of Ogham is, along with the flowers and herbs we mentioned in previous chapters, an aspect of the theory of correspondences. These different trees allow you to incorporate seasonal elements into your ceremony, perhaps in the form of a ritual wand or perhaps simply as boughs and garlands. All these trees are symbolic and give you the opportunity to bring classic pagan elements into your ceremony.

Conclusion

Throughout this book, I have attempted to cover as many questions as I can relating to your handfasting: the history, practicalities, logistics, and magic of your big day. A handfasting ritual, as we have seen, is a wonderful way to make a commitment, either for a lifetime or simply for a year and a day, but handfasting is not just about the ritual itself: there is magic to be undertaken both before and after the ceremony. Placing your faith and trust in the gods and goddesses of love and marriage will help both your big day and your lives together run smoothly—but the gods notoriously help those who help themselves! Preparation and forethought, both about the ceremony itself and the magical practices surrounding it, will ensure that you have a truly memorable and wonderful experience. Blessed be!

Resources

https://www.gq-magazine.co.uk/lifestyle/article/how-to-propose

https://www.theknot.com/content/romantic-ways-to-propose

https://cocoweddingvenues.co.uk

https://www.ukawp.com

https://www.paganfed.org

https://www.facebook.com/cwasask/ (CWAS—Congregationalist Wiccan Association of Saskatchewan)

http://cwabc.org (CWAS—Congregationalist Wiccan Association of British Colombia)

https://druidnetwork.org/what-is-druidry/rites-and-rituals/rites-passage/rites-marriage-handfasting/ (This gives some examples of handfasting rituals.)

Invitations

http://www.hedinghamfair.co.uk/wedding_invitations.htm

Celebrants

www.witchcraftshop.co.uk (Liz Williams and Trevor Jones)

www.spiritualorkney.co.uk

http://goddesstempleweddings.co.uk

https://officiantdirectory.com (For the US)

Cords

https://officiantdirectory.com/ultimate-handfasting-guide/ (This is for the US. As well as cords, it also contains some ideas about writing your vows and other helpful information.)

Ideas for Poems and Readings

https://www.youandyourwedding.co.uk/ideas-and-advice/readings-and-speeches/readings-and-poems-for-civil-ceremonies/

Bibliography

Alcock, Jayne. *The Language of Flowers*. Bridgwater: Bridgwater College, 2016.

Anton, Alexander. *Handfasting in Scotland: The Scottish Historical Review*. Edinburgh, UK: Edinburgh University Press, 1958.

Carr-Gomm, Philip, and Stephanie Carr-Gomm. *Druid Plant Oracle*. London: Saint Martin's Press, 2007.

Chapman, Bernadette. "UK Alliance of Wedding Planners." https://www.ukawp.com.

Cortambert, Louise. *Le Langage des Fleurs*. Paris: Audot, 1834.

Craigie, William. *The Dictionary of Older Scottish Tongue*. Dundee: University of Dundee, 1931–2002.

Crowley, Aleister. *The Confessions of Aleister Crowley*. New York: Penguin, 1979.

Drayton, Michael. *The Folk-Lore Journal*. Abingdon, 1885.

Eska, Charlene. *Cáin Lánamna: An Old Irish Tract on Marriage and Divorce Law*. Leiden: Brill, 2009.

Evelyn-White, Hugh G. *The Homeric Hymns and Homerica*. London: William Heinemann, 1914.

Faraone, Christopher. "Ancient Greek Love Magic." *Fathom Archive*. Accessed November 3, 2020. http://fathom.lib.uchicago.edu/1/777777122299/.

Fitch, Ed. "Traditional Pagan Blessing, Spiritual Love Poems and Readings." Accessed November 3, 2020. https://www.churchofancientways.org.

Flood, Gavin. Interview with the *Guardian*. September 21, 2020.

Fosse, Lars Martin. *The Kamasutra*. Woodstock: YogaVidya, 2012.

Frazer, James George. *The Golden Bough*. London: Macmillan, 1890.

Greenaway, Kate. *The Language of Flowers*. London: George Routledge and Sons, 1884.

Hill, Simone. "66 Proposal Ideas to Spark Romance." *The Knot*. Accessed November 3, 2020. https://www.theknot.com/content/romantic-ways-to-propose.

Homer. *Iliad: Book XIV*. Translated by E. V. Rieu. London: Penguin, 1950.

Hymn to Hathor. "The Faery's Gifts." Accessed November 3, 2020. https://murfeelee.tumblr.com/post/157820672285/.

Kaldera, Raven, and Tannin Schwartzstein. *Inviting Hera's Blessing: Handfasting and Wedding Rituals*. Woodbury: Llewellyn, 2003.

Martin, Martin. *A Description of the Western Islands of Scotland*. Cornhil: A. Bell, 1776.

Myers, Justin. "How to Propose." Accessed November 3, 2020. https://www.gq-magazine.co.uk/lifestyle/article/how-to-propose.

Newsroom. "The origins of handfasting at Scottish weddings—When Scots 'married' for a year and a day." *Scotsman*. Accessed November 3, 2020. https://www.scotsman.com/regions/origins-handfasting-scottish-weddings-when-scots-married-year-and-day-113813.

Nicholl, Charles. "The Lodger Shakespeare: His Life on Silver Street." https://erenow.net/biographies/the-lodger-shakespeare-his-life-on-silver-street.

Otter, Katrina. "Hiring a Wedding Planner—Who, What, Why, When & Where." January 2017. https://cocoweddingvenues.co.uk.

Ovid. *Fasti: Book IV*. Edited by Elaine Fantham. Cambridge: Cambidge University Press, 1998.

Pennant, Thomas. *Tour in Scotland*. London: B. White, 1776.

Phillips, Henry. *Floral Emblems*. London: Sanders and Otley, 1825.

Pollock, Frederick, and Frederic Maitland. *History of English Law.* Indianapolis: Liberty Fund, 2010.

Randolph, Paschal Beverly. *Eulis! The History of Love.* Toledo: Randolph Publishing Co., 1874.

Scott, Walter. *The Monastery.* Edinburgh: Constable and Ballantyne, 1820.

The Scots Magazine. Dundee: University of Dundee, 1933.

Sinclair, John. *The [Old] Statistical Account of Scotland.* Edinburgh: William Creech, 1791–99.

Sophistes, Apollonius. "Homeric Hymn to Aphrodite." Translated by Gregory Nagy. Accessed November 3, 2020. https://uh.edu/~cldue/texts/aphrodite.html.

Strayer, Joseph R., ed. "Ormulum." In *Dictionary of the Middle Ages.* New York: Charles Scribner's Sons, 1987.

Sweeney, Ray. "Pagan Federation of Ireland—the Ray Sweeney interview." *Languageofmoons.* Accessed November 3, 2020. https://languageofmoons.wordpress.com/2010/06/20/pagan-federation-of-ireland-the-ray-sweeney-interview/.

Swinburne, Henry. *Treatise of Spousals.* London: Daniel Brown, Thomas Ward, and William Mears, 1711.

von Hammer-Purgstall, Joseph. *Dictionnaire du langage des fleurs.* Paris: Annales des voyages, 1809.

Waterman Esling, Catharine H. *Flora's Lexicon.* Philadelphia: Herman Hooker, 1839.

Webster, John. *The Duchess of Malfi.* London: Okes, 1612–13.

Wordsworth, William. "Resolution and Independence." *Poetry Foundation.* Accessed November 3, 2020. https://www.poetryfoundation.org/poems/45545/resolution-and-independence.

To Write to the Author

If you wish to contact the author or would like more information about this book, please write to the author in care of Llewellyn Worldwide Ltd. and we will forward your request. Both the author and the publisher appreciate hearing from you and learning of your enjoyment of this book and how it has helped you. Llewellyn Worldwide Ltd. cannot guarantee that every letter written to the author can be answered, but all will be forwarded. Please write to:

Liz Williams
℅ Llewellyn Worldwide
2143 Wooddale Drive
Woodbury, MN 55125-2989

Please enclose a self-addressed stamped envelope for reply,
or $1.00 to cover costs. If outside the U.S.A., enclose
an international postal reply coupon.

Many of Llewellyn's authors have websites with additional information and resources. For more information, please visit our website at http://www.llewellyn.com.